World Hunger

Look for these and other books in the Lucent
Overview series:

World Hunger

by Liza N. Burby

LUCENT
B·O·O·K·S

Library of Congress Cataloging-in-Publication Data

Burby, Liza N.
    World hunger / by Liza N. Burby.
        p.   cm. — (Lucent overview series)
    Includes bibliographical references and index.
    ISBN 1-56006-120-0
    1. Food supply—Juvenile literature.   2. Malnutrition—Juvenile
literature.   3. Famines—Juvenile literature.   4. Starvation—
Juvenile literature.   [1. Hunger.   2. Food supply.   3. Famines.]
I. Title.   II. Series.
HD9000.5.B86   1995
363.8—dc20   94-16830
                                                       CIP
                                                        AC

© Copyright 1995 by Lucent Books, Inc.
P.O. Box 289011, San Diego, CA 92198-9011
Printed in the U.S.A.

Contents

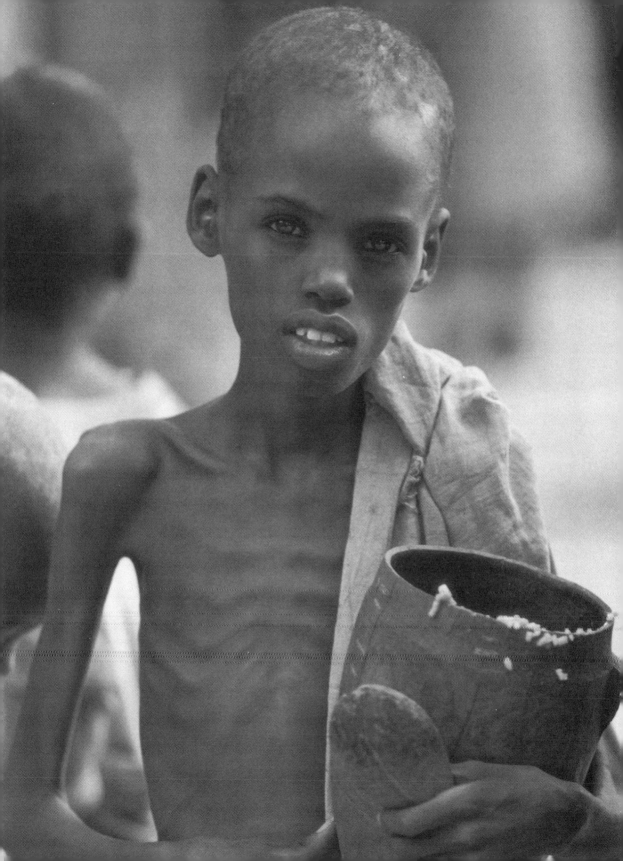

Introduction

THERE HAS PROBABLY never been a time in human history when hunger did not exist. Paleolithic bone remains show that people as long ago as 4000 B.C. had bouts of stunted growth, which indicates periods of a lack of food. Scientists today believe changes in the availability of plants, animals, and fish caused seasonal hunger. In other words, during different times of the year the weather may have affected food supplies. Historians believe that during the Middle Ages famine, or widespread hunger, swept across Europe every ten years. Perhaps the most famous famine occurred between 1845 and 1847 in Ireland. A blight, or disease, devastated potatoes, which was the staple crop of the Irish. An estimated 1.5 million people starved to death.

Hunger in modern times

While there is nothing new about hunger and starvation, today it is a problem that affects people worldwide from wealthy nations such as the United States to poor nations such as those in Africa. Natural disasters like drought and human actions such as war have caused widespread hunger and famine in many nations in the last thirty years.

(Opposite page) A young Somali boy is luckier than many—he was able to make it to a Red Cross food distribution point for some much-needed rice and beans.

An estimated 1.5 million people starved to death during the Irish potato famine. Here, starving Irish citizens stand at the gate of the workhouse in hopes of finding food.

The first modern food crisis occurred in 1967 when a two-year drought struck most of Asia, causing a harvest shortfall of nearly thirty million tons of grain. That year the Indian government and international agencies organized one of the biggest programs of disaster relief undertaken up until that time. It relied mostly on wheat shipments from the United States, which helped stave off starvation among India's people. In the northeast Indian state of Bihar alone, six million children and women were fed by food relief each day. It is believed that this prevented what might have been one of the worst famines in history.

India's brush with almost certain catastrophe focused public attention on world hunger and world food production. Scientists introduced the Green Revolution, through which new varieties of wheat and rice dramatically increased crop yields and appeared to signal an end to hunger. The successes of the Green Revolution were short-lived, however. By the 1970s news of crop failures, famines, and shrinking grain reserves worldwide again filled the media.

What hunger experts have observed since then is that the roots of hunger run deeper than crop yields and scientific discoveries. While science and agriculture have much to offer, they cannot end hunger alone, for the nature of hunger has changed from crisis-driven food shortages to chronic, or constant, food poverty. Though crises still do lead to hunger, sometimes on a large scale, hunger has taken hold in a more permanent way in many parts of the world. This means that individual households cannot meet their food

Starving Indians sit at a relief station in Bihar in 1967. Considered the first modern food crisis, the famine led to the largest international relief effort up to that point in time.

needs despite adequate food supplies in their countries. Chronic food hunger is persisting, and in some cases increasing.

The current status of world food supply, demand, and distribution is a complex one. It involves economics, politics, and the environment. Hunger is not a problem of too little food to go around. Rather, it is a problem of getting food to the people who need it the most. Hunger is also not a concern limited only to those people who are living through it. The hunger issue is a global one. People from all nations have been striving for decades to find solutions to the problem of hunger.

A world goal of food security

Since the mid-1970s governments and aid groups worldwide have named food security as an international goal. Food security, in this case,

Today, relief efforts are usually international in scope and are directed by the United Nations.

means access to enough food so that all people can maintain healthy, active lives.

In 1974 U.S. secretary of state Dr. Henry Kissinger told gatherers at a world food conference: "Today we must proclaim a bold objective: that within a decade, no child will go to bed hungry, and that no family will fear for its next day's bread and that no human being's future and capacity will be stunted by malnutrition." Ten years later a United Nations report indicated that over the last decade the number of hungry people had roughly doubled to 450 million people.

However, since then some countries that experienced severe hunger problems in the past, such as China, Korea, and Taiwan, have eliminated hunger through controlling population growth and by improving economic conditions. Modern technology and increased understanding of the issues surrounding hunger have made food experts hopeful that hunger can be ended in other countries in the future. In a 1994 interview with the author, Robert W. Kates, past director of the World Hunger Program at Brown University, said:

> Despite the long-term persistence of hunger, for the first time the end of food scarcity, famine, and mass starvation looks like an attainable future goal. But it will require complex and difficult choices at many levels of human action and organization.

1

A Global Problem

HUNGER IN ITS most extreme form is a weakened condition brought about by a prolonged lack of food. Without food the body is deprived of the nutrients it needs for growth and health. The result is often starvation. Persistent hunger keeps people from working productively and thinking clearly. It decreases their resistance to disease. It can also be extremely painful. Further, it has the potential to cause permanent damage to the brain as well as to the body. If hunger continues long enough, it results in death.

The Great Hunger Belt

Currently, twenty million people, including fifteen million children, die each year from starvation and related illnesses. In other words, over forty-one thousand deaths a day are caused by hunger.

These statistics are not confined to any one region of the world. Hunger is considered a global problem, one that afflicts Peru as well as the Sudan, and Southeast Asia as well as the Saharan region of Africa. Hunger also exists in some industrialized countries like the United States where an estimated thirty million people do not always have enough to eat. Yet the majority of the world's hungry people live in what is known as the Great

(Opposite page) Starving women hold their hungry children during a famine in Ethiopia. Ethiopia is one of the many countries located in an area known as the Great Hunger Belt.

13

Hunger Belt: Southeast Asia through India and its surrounding countries, known as the Indian subcontinent, the Middle East, and throughout the continent of Africa and parts of Latin America.

These countries are also referred to as Third World, or developing, countries. The United Nations classifies 141 African, Asian, and Latin American countries as Third World countries. They are considered developing countries because they have high illiteracy rates, high birth rates, limited schools, and crude communication and transportation systems, and they cannot meet their food needs.

Almost 57 percent of the world's chronically hungry people live in Asia. Chronic hunger—a long-term lack of the proteins and calories needed for survival—is concentrated especially in the seven countries of southern Asia: Bangladesh, Bhutan, India, Maldives, Nepal, Pakistan, and Sri Lanka. More than half of the world's hungry people live in India, a country that is one-third the

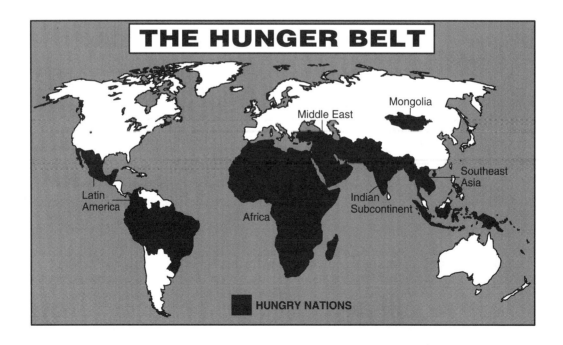

THE HUNGER BELT

Mongolia

Middle East

Southeast Asia

Latin America

Indian Subcontinent

Africa

■ HUNGRY NATIONS

Children await meals in India, where more than half of the world's hungry people live. The average Indian child is given 8,530 government-sponsored meals before reaching school age.

size of the United States. Nations are viewed as experiencing chronic hunger when 25 percent or more of their children under the age of four are seriously underweight. In southern Asia, for example, 108 million children, or 63 percent, are underweight. A six-month-old baby who weighs less than thirteen pounds would be considered underweight because healthy six-month-old babies average seventeen pounds, and many weigh more than that. The underweight baby probably gets less than 80 percent of the recommended calorie intake for a child of that age. With so few nutrients in its diet, that baby would probably also be classified as malnourished, or suffering from malnutrition.

Malnutrition is a potentially fatal condition that occurs when a person has too few of the nutrients needed for good health and normal body functions. Malnutrition and chronic hunger are so closely linked that one usually accompanies the other. "Today, between 700 million to one billion people suffer from persistent and chronic hunger and malnutrition," says Ismail Serageldin, a vice president of the World Bank, which lends funds to the governments of developing nations.

Malnutrition and chronic hunger

Malnutrition is most common in regions of the world where chronic hunger is also a problem. Malnutrition affects 188 million children in the developing countries. Eighty-three percent of those children live in Asia. In Latin America and the Caribbean malnutrition is considered to be the main cause of 60 percent of the deaths of children under the age of five.

Bangladesh is one of the countries whose population suffers from chronic hunger and malnutrition. Bordered by India and Myanmar (formerly Burma), two countries that also have severe hunger problems, Bangladesh is one of the poorest countries in the world. The majority of its more than 104 million people suffer from chronic hunger and malnutrition. With malnutrition affecting 65 percent of its children, Bangladesh has the highest rate of malnutrition in the world.

While a large percentage of the world's chronically hungry people live in Asia, many suffer in other regions of the world too. The Bread for the World Institute, an organization that educates people about hunger, classifies numerous other countries as experiencing chronic hunger. The organization's list includes Myanmar, Laos, Vietnam, Thailand, Cambodia, Indonesia, Papua New Guinea, and the Philippines, all in Southeast Asia; Guatemala in Central America; Iran and Yemen in the Middle East; and Mali, Niger, Nigeria, Ghana,

Congo, Mauritania, Liberia, Namibia, Madagascar, Tanzania, and Rwanda, all in Africa.

Africa is the region where hunger is growing most rapidly. Over the last thirty years, twenty-nine of thirty-six countries in the desert region known as the Sahel, or sub-Saharan Africa, have been hit with food shortages. In 1992 drought and wars placed about sixty million Africans at risk of starvation. That total included fifty-three million in northeastern and southern Africa.

One-quarter of Africa's population is threatened by chronic food shortages. According to the United Nations Children's Fund (UNICEF), an organization that helps countries improve their

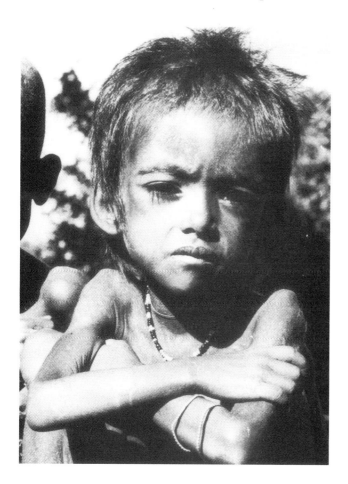

A starving child in Bangladesh awaits her next meal at a relief camp. Bangladesh has the highest malnutrition rate in the world.

health services for children, the number of families who are unable to meet their basic food needs doubled in the last decade. This led to a rising number of malnourished children. Because they also had limited access to health services and clean water, increasing the likelihood of infectious diseases, Africa's people experienced the highest infant mortality, or deaths, and lowest life expectancy worldwide. Unemployment and underemployment increased. The U.N. Food and Agricultural Organization (FAO) projects that there will be 200 million hungry and malnourished Africans by the year 2000.

Chronic hunger is one of the most troubling forms of hunger because it is long lasting and usually deeply enmeshed in the history, politics, economics, and social structure of a country. A country's job base, wage levels, educational and business opportunities, local and national leadership, past associations with other nations, and religious and cultural customs may all play a part in leading to and doing away with chronic hunger. Change does not come easily in any of these areas, which is why chronic hunger is difficult to eliminate. Not all countries with hunger problems suffer from chronic hunger, however. There are other forms of hunger, and some of these are considered easier to reduce or eliminate than chronic hunger.

Famine

Famine is one such form of hunger. Famine is a scarcity of food that puts large portions of a population in danger of dying from starvation. It is usually brought on by a sudden or temporary crisis like flooding or war. But it may also result from ongoing conditions such as drought or a combination of sudden and ongoing events. When a crisis occurs, a population may be unable to get food supplies. Sometimes this is because

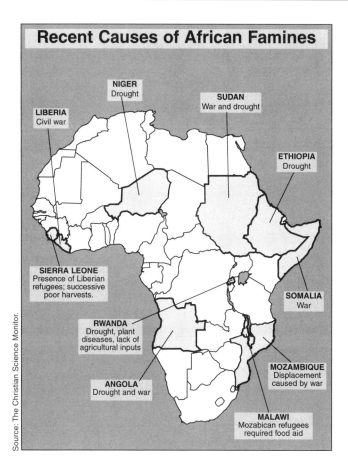

Recent Causes of African Famines

NIGER
Drought

LIBERIA
Civil war

SUDAN
War and drought

ETHIOPIA
Drought

SIERRA LEONE
Presence of Liberian
refugees; successive
poor harvests.

SOMALIA
War

RWANDA
Drought, plant
diseases, lack of
agricultural inputs

MOZAMBIQUE
Displacement
caused by war

ANGOLA
Drought and war

MALAWI
Mozabican refugees
required food aid

Source: The Christian Science Monitor.

the food has been destroyed by a natural event like a flash flood. Sometimes it occurs because armed conflict blocks food distribution.

Most of the recent famines have occurred in Africa in countries whose governments have been involved in civil war. In 1988 alone, according to Brown University's *1989 Hunger Report*, famines occurred in at least five countries having a combined population of 205 million, or 4 percent of the world's population. War was the most frequent cause of these famines. In 1987 wars were fought in twenty-three countries in Africa. In seventeen of those countries food-growing and distribution systems were disrupted. Armed conflict in the southern Sudan caused about 260,000 people to

Somali refugee children receive milk at a food distribution center after civil war brought widespread famine to the area.

die of starvation in 1988 and 1989 when food aid shipments were blocked by the military there.

Although famine is a serious problem that can devastate whole populations, it is easier to end than chronic hunger because it can usually be solved with emergency food aid. "If not for armed conflict," says Robert W. Kates, former director of the World Hunger Program at Brown University, "famine worldwide could be eliminated. All of the mechanisms are in place to end famine. We know how to deal with it because there is a very extensive international food emergency system in place to deliver food almost anywhere."

Such an emergency system was used in the African nation of Somalia, where war-driven famine killed thousands of people. Somalia, a crescent-shaped country of 8.3 million people, was embroiled in civil war between 1991 and 1994. Although war was the primary cause of famine in Somalia, a severe drought deepened the crisis. Few of the crops that were planted in 1991 survived the prolonged dry spell that ended in 1992. When the rains came, only about 5 percent of the crops were able to be harvested because of the fighting, which often took place on farmlands. The violence of war also prevented the people from importing the food they needed to avert famine and hampered relief efforts from the Red Cross and other organizations. The United Nations estimated that only half of the food aid shipped there reached the hungry. The rest had been looted and sold for profit or used to feed the gangs who stole it. In all, more than 350,000 Somalis died as a result of famine in that three-year period.

U.N. troops landed in the country in early 1993 to make sure that food supplies reached the hungry. Within a few months the famine was almost over. According to a March 26, 1994, *New York Times* article, aid agencies distributed $62 million worth of food. UNICEF, the largest relief agency in Somalia, was also able to vaccinate 753,000 children, build 3,700 wells, and bring 62,000 children back to school. Farmers were also able to return to their fields under military protection.

At risk of famine

While progress has been made, there is more work to be done in Somalia. It is considered a country still at risk of famine because continuing political unrest and outbreaks of violence threaten the country's ability to produce or import enough food for the population. Until stability returns to Somalia, aid agencies will probably continue to provide food relief in hopes of avoiding famine.

Other countries are also considered to be on the verge of famine. These include Haiti in the Caribbean, Peru in South America, Afghanistan

Somalis pass Nigerian soldiers in a U.N. armored vehicle in central Mogadishu. Once U.N. troops went into the area, the famine was ended quickly.

and Iraq in the Middle East, and Sierra Leone, Angola, Zimbabwe, Rwanda, and Ethiopia in Africa. Different events have pushed each of these countries ever closer to famine, just as several events combined in Mozambique in the early 1990s to put that country at risk of famine.

Malawi, a nation of 8.8 million people in eastern Africa, endured a drought from 1990 to 1992. As a result of the drought and frequent riots to overthrow the regime of Malawi's president, Hastings Banda, food production plummeted. The country also served as host to almost a million refugees from neighboring Mozambique, which was engulfed in civil war until 1994. This put further pressure on Malawi's limited food supplies. Mozambican refugees are now trickling back to their homeland. While hunger could have become a serious problem in Malawi, where most of the population lives in poverty, the government did not have to seek food relief because the people were still able to feed the population from the country's own crops.

Similarities among the hungry

While the causes of hunger differ in each country, all countries suffering from hunger—especially chronic hunger—share one characteristic: poverty. Most of the nations whose people suffer from chronic hunger are poor. Their hunger comes mostly from inadequate income rather than from a shortage of world food supplies. Many of them must spend about 80 percent of their income on food, which provides them with only about 80 percent of what they need to maintain a healthy diet.

The statistics for hunger and poverty are so closely connected that they are almost the same. About 750 million of the world's people live in

Mozambican refugees in Malawi. Although Malawi is a poor, underdeveloped nation, it has sufficient stability to be able to feed its people and the refugees who flooded into the area.

absolute poverty. This means that they are unable to grow enough food or earn enough money to supply their basic needs. The people who suffer from chronic hunger worldwide are also among the world's poorest people. "Hunger," writes the World Bank's Serageldin, "is the most extreme form of poverty."

Most victims of hunger in any region can be found in households that depend on low-wage, labor-intensive jobs like making crafts, or day-labor construction jobs for their income. They live in households that have poor land to farm, or none at all, and especially in households headed by women, which tend to be the poorest. The percentage of women-headed households is growing rapidly as men move to cities in search of work. Women now manage alone in 40 percent of the households in some parts of rural Africa. In other

Afghan refugees run a small workshop to supplement their income. Self-employed crafts-men are the most likely to fall victim to hunger.

regions the percentage of women-headed households ranges from 10 to 30 percent.

Even for those living in the same household, the extent of hunger often differs from one person to another because of a lack of education about proper nutrition and because of cultural beliefs. Many women unknowingly neglect the nutritional needs of their children and themselves, particularly when they are pregnant or breast-feeding. As a result, 30 percent of African women suffer from anemia, a blood deficiency that weakens them. This causes many of their children to have low birth weight and to suffer from malnutrition by the time they are two, according to UNICEF.

In many poor families men and boys eat, even when others go hungry. Many cultures believe it is more important for males to eat first because they earn an income. Therefore, women and girls typically suffer more severe malnutrition than do men and boys. About 40 percent of the world's hungry people are children; most of the rest are women. Further, four times more malnourished children are female than male.

The World Bank and other organizations have made reduction of poverty a main goal for Third World countries. By lessening poverty, Serageldin says, hunger, too, will decrease. The two are so closely intertwined that one can hardly be changed without altering the other.

2

What Are the Effects of Hunger?

HUNGER LEAVES MANY extreme and often unbearable conditions in its wake. While most of the initial impacts of hunger relate to an individual's health, long-term hunger can also affect a country's social, economic, and political life. Therefore, it causes a chain of events that influences not only an individual's present health, but also the health of future generations.

When a person experiences long-term hunger, the body becomes undernourished and weak. Undernourishment occurs when a person does not eat enough calories of energy-producing food to lead a normal life. The U.S. government estimates that the average adult's energy requirements are 2,400 calories a day. However, the average inactive adult could survive on 1,600 calories a day. But even this figure is far more than what most people in Third World countries eat. For example, in Calcutta, India, four out of five people get less than 900 calories' worth of food a day. The human body does not run solely on calories, but also on at least forty-five essential nutrients. A malnourished person lacks not only the proper

(Opposite page) Biafran refugee children from Nigeria are cared for at the French Army Field Hospital. Most of the children are suffering from malnutrition.

27

amount of food, but also the quality of food needed to maintain good health. The approximately one billion malnourished people in the world are at risk of poor health because they do not get key nutrients, such as fat, protein, carbohydrates, vitamins, and minerals.

When a person is healthy, the body stores extra food as fat. Most people have enough fat so that their health would not be damaged if they went several days without food. However, when a person does not have fat stores, food deprivation becomes serious because the body starts to consume proteins that are stored in the muscles and organs. This is the beginning of starvation. Starvation is the extreme form of malnourishment in which the body begins to devour vital tissues. Eventually organs such as the liver and the brain begin to break down until they stop functioning. This is death by starvation.

Hunger-related diseases

However, most hunger-related deaths are probably from disease rather than from starvation. People who are suffering from malnutrition are more prone to become sick and die of even common illnesses, such as diarrhea, because their bodies are too weak to resist infection. In the crowded and unsanitary conditions usually found in regions where hunger persists, individuals often do not get a chance to recuperate from one infection before they are hit with another. Every bout with disease further weakens the body until it can no longer function. This is when death results.

Malnourished people suffer from one or many deficiency diseases, which are diseases caused by a lack of essential nutrients, especially vitamins and minerals. Kwashiorkor is one such disease. It is one of the most widespread dietary diseases in the world. Kwashiorkor is caused by not enough

A father in eastern Sudan walks toward a refugee camp while carrying his son, who is dying of malnutrition.

protein and too many carbohydrates in the diet. It mostly affects children, especially when they are being weaned from breast milk. Young children need large amounts of various proteins for growth and many body functions. Breast milk contains proteins that the body needs for normal development but which it either cannot make or cannot make in sufficient amounts. However, the proteins in breast milk protect against deficiency only if the basic diet is reasonably adequate. But the basic diet is often inadequate in the world's poorest regions. In many places children eat only starchy foods that are low in protein and high in carbohydrates, and this can lead to kwashiorkor. Often the starchy foods do not have as many proteins as breast milk. Children with kwashiorkor in

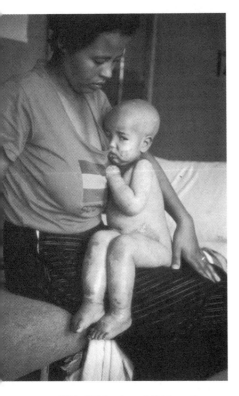

This Ethiopian child has the typical symptoms of kwashiorkor—his skin has swelled and lost its color.

Jamaica, for example, were called "sugar babies," because they got plenty of calories, but no protein, from eating sugar. This caused people to think that sugar caused the disease.

Kwashiorkor stops or slows down a baby's growth. In severe cases the muscles waste away and the skin swells with body fluids. As the disease worsens, the skin loses its natural color and may develop dark patches, and black hair sometimes turns reddish brown. Kwashiorkor also damages the liver and the small intestine, leaving the body susceptible to other, sometimes fatal infections. Although kwashiorkor can be treated with dried skim, or nonfat, milk and other high-protein food supplements, the disease is often fatal because treatment is frequently unavailable. Children who recover from the disease usually do not grow fully.

It is not just a shortage of protein-rich food that can cause people to become sick from malnourishment. The human body also needs minerals, vitamins, and other nutrients. In the developing world foods containing these essential nutrients are not always available. Iron and iodine are two examples. Iron and iodine deficiencies affect at least 500 million people.

Iron and iodine deficiencies

Iron deficiency is the most common nutrient shortage in the world today. Two-thirds of the population in developing countries has an iron-deficient diet. Iron is found in body organs that form and destroy blood cells. Small amounts of iron are needed in all body cells, however, as well as in muscles and other tissues. Iron forms an essential part of a substance called hemoglobin, which carries oxygen from the lungs to other body tissues. Hemoglobin also carries carbon dioxide away from tissues to the lungs, where it is expelled from the body. A shortage of iron slows down a person's brain functions, making learning and physical activity slower. It also hampers the substances in the body that kill bacteria. An iron supplement is all that is needed to prevent this from happening, but even this is not available to many people in poor countries.

Iodine deficiency is another common disorder among people in Third World countries. People need only a teaspoonful of iodine in their whole lifetime. Without it growth is stunted, and movement, speech, and hearing are impaired. Iodine is normally found in fish and foods grown in iodine-rich soil. However, one-fifth of the world's population lives in places where iodine has been washed from the soil because of flooding or erosion. In these areas many people have developed goiter, a swelling of the thyroid gland in the neck. Adding iodine to salt supplies is a way to end goiter. Iodine deficiency also causes miscarriages, stillbirths, and infant and child deaths. It also

People such as this woman, who received insufficient amounts of iodine, develop goiter, or swelling of the thyroid gland.

causes cretinism, a condition in which babies are born with underdeveloped brains and poorly formed skeletons. About 800 million people worldwide are at risk of iodine deficiency, with 190 million suffering from goiter, and 3 million from cretinism.

Vitamin A deficiencies

Health problems related to vitamin A deficiencies are common in about thirty-seven countries, including some of the most populous nations of Asia, Africa, and Latin America. Vitamin A promotes good vision and helps form and maintain skin, teeth, bones, and mucous membranes. A lack of vitamin A can cause problems for people of all ages, but the most vulnerable are young children and women who are pregnant or breast-feeding.

Worldwide about forty million preschool children suffer from some degree of vitamin A deficiency. The most common outcome of this disorder is blindness, since severe vitamin A deficiency damages parts of the eye, beginning with the cornea. Almost forty thousand children go blind each year from a lack of vitamin A. Before permanent blindness sets in, many of them suffer from night blindness, which means they cannot see in the dark. Besides keeping eyes healthy, vitamin A also helps keep the passages to the lungs and stomach healthy. When these passages are not well, they cannot protect the body from infection. This leads to respiratory illnesses, such as pneumonia and whooping cough, and to diarrhea. Vitamin A deficiency can easily be avoided if people eat foods like liver, milk, eggs, carrots, spinach, and mangoes. However these foods are not readily available in all countries whose populations are coping with malnutrition.

Malnutrition can also lead to diarrhea, which is an intestinal condition leading to frequent and loose bowel movements. Diarrheal disease is the number one cause of illness and death among children under five. It is not diarrhea itself but dehydration, or the loss of water in the body, that kills four million children each year. Frequent bouts of diarrhea drain too much liquid and nutrients from a child's body so that it becomes dehydrated and malnourished. It is easy to prevent dehydration if parents are able to give their children plenty of liquids to drink, such as breast milk, soup, tea, and water. But in poor countries not only are adequate food supplies lacking, very often so is clean water. A simple, inexpensive technique known as oral rehydration technique, or ORT, has reduced the childhood death rate from diarrheal disease to about three million. With ORT, a person drinks a prepared mixture of sugar, salts, and water that replaces the fluids lost through diarrhea. Each ORT beverage packet costs about ten cents.

Effects on women and children

Disease is one terrible result of hunger, but hunger has other effects on the body's ability to function normally. Pregnant and breast-feeding women and children under the age of five are often identified as groups that are especially vulnerable to hunger. In the extremes of malnutrition a woman may not be able to become pregnant or carry a baby to term, or a full nine months. This happens because the fetus depends solely on the mother's food intake for the nutrients it needs to grow. If the mother eats too little or no food, like a seed without water, the fetus cannot thrive. Even with less-extreme deprivation, if a woman does not have enough to eat during pregnancy, the development of her baby can be impaired, perhaps permanently. Poor maternal nutrition during pregnancy can cause low birth weight in the baby. In southern Asia, for example, 30 percent of all babies are underweight at birth. This is the highest figure in any one region in the world.

Babies who weigh very little at birth—less than five pounds—are at increased risk of dying in infancy, because their bodies are nutrient deficient. A baby who survives is more likely to suffer from an underdeveloped immune system, which can cause respiratory disorders. The digestive system might also be impaired. The infant might have a short attention span and be unable to tolerate stimulation, such as being sung to or played with, which is how a healthy baby learns. Further, a baby who is weak at birth may be unable to breast-feed. This seriously decreases its chances of survival.

However, the female body is sometimes surprisingly able to carry a baby to term, deliver a healthy baby, and give that baby high-quality milk even if the mother is malnourished. But if a woman does this, she weakens the nutritional supplies of her own body. If she becomes pregnant again without building up her nutrients she can develop anemia, a condition in which the blood cannot provide the body tissues with enough oxygen, and eventually die.

Essential nourishment

A mother's breast milk is essential for the healthy development of children because it contains all the nutrients their bodies need. Malnourished children do not grow properly. Even if malnutrition lasts a short time, a child's growth can be stunted. To ensure good nutrition, as well as to provide natural immunities against infections and diarrhea, children need only breast milk for the first six months of life. Calorie requirements for young children are as low as 800 a day, but those who deteriorate from malnutrition need supple-

An Ethiopian baby is weighed in at a refugee camp. A high percentage of Ethiopians suffer from malnutrition, which especially affects small children.

People shield their faces from the sun as they wait for food at a famine relief center.

ments to catch up on growth. Until they are three years old, children need to eat five or six times a day, twice as often as adults, and they need at least small amounts of oils, fats, and vegetables.

Because most of a child's brain cell development occurs before the second birthday, proper nutrition is very important in the early years of life. A child who falls behind in brain development cannot make it up. Even a few months of malnutrition in infancy can mean below-average intelligence levels. This can affect memory, attention span, and speech and language skills.

A priority of survival

In adults the most immediate effect of sustained hunger is lack of energy, or listlessness. Malnourished adults are often too weak to work and so cannot earn the money or grow the food needed for their own or their family's survival. An undernourished worker needs to work fewer days and must take frequent breaks while working. Nevin S. Scrimshaw, director of the Food and Nutrition Program of the United Nations University, said that in much of Central America

Boys transplant seedlings of rice in an irrigated field in Mali during a drought. Constant hunger and malnutrition can make children and adults sluggish and unable to work.

plantation workers are paid by the task rather than by the hour because there is so much variation in the amount of work that a poorly nourished laborer can complete in an hour on the job.

When children are hungry, they, too, are not very active. This means they do not play as much or have the opportunity for exploration and social interaction, all of which are important for intellectual and social development. Many do not have the opportunity to go to school, either because they are too weak to attend or because school is not a priority in homes where people are committed to finding enough food just to survive. Young people in some countries must stay home to care for younger brothers and sisters, tend livestock and animals, and fetch water and fuel. In rural Bangladesh, for instance, young girls help their mothers clean house, prepare food, and tend the garden, while young boys help their fathers plow, plant, and harvest crops. All of these activities can help keep a family alive.

However, when children do not have the opportunity to go to school, they are more likely to start families at a young age. This increases the risk that their own children will be malnourished. Education is strongly related to better levels of child health and nutrition and lower levels of pregnancy and infant deaths. In Pakistan uneducated women are three times more likely to have malnourished children than those women with at least an elementary school education. On average, every additional year a mother spends in school decreases infant deaths by approximately nine for every thousand children. Without some schooling a mother will be illiterate, or unable to read. This plays out in dangerous ways for her children if she cannot read labels on food packages, for instance, or cannot even read a sign that tells her where she can get medicine for her children. For those who do not attend school, the greater risk is that hunger will continue within these families for many generations to come.

Desperate measures

The survival instinct is so strong that people who experience hunger may take desperate measures to stay alive. Often such measures only prolong hunger. Hunger experts have witnessed this type of behavior in countries around the world. When people run out of food, for example, their

A key to good nutrition is education. These Afghan refugee children in Pakistan are provided with schooling as part of the nation's humanitarian assistance program.

38

first step is to sell everything they own—land, water rights, trees, and livestock. They use this money to buy food supplies. When that money runs out, they often end up eating the seeds they would have used for the next year's planting. This pattern occurs frequently in Ethiopia, an eastern African country that suffers a food emergency every two years, says Robert Buchanan, a Washington, D.C., representative of OXFAM America, an international development and relief organization. When no food remains, the next step is to move to nearby towns and cities to search for work or to obtain food charity.

Hunger among refugees

This effect of hunger is called migration, and those who leave one area to search for food in another become refugees. Individual families may migrate, but more commonly in times of severe drought or warfare, whole communities and villages will migrate. Sometimes they move to other parts of their own country, and often to neighboring countries. In 1994 there were eleven countries in which people became refugees within their own countries or crossed the border into other countries. These are Bosnia and Croatia in East-

An Ethiopian refugee cooks wild grasses for food in a refugee camp in Sudan.

ern Europe, Tajikistan, Afghanistan, and Iraq in the Middle East, and Angola, Burundi, Liberia, Mozambique, Rwanda, and Somalia in Africa.

The U.N. High Commission for Refugees says that the number of refugees crossing borders has mushroomed over the last twenty years, from 2.4 million in 1974 to 10.5 million by 1984 to close to 23 million in 1994. When added to the estimated 26 million internally displaced people, that total reaches a staggering 49 million. That means that, for various reasons including hunger, one of every 114 people in the world has been uprooted and forced to move somewhere else. This is part of a growing trend worldwide as people flee their homes from famine and war.

Migration often does not mean the end of starvation for the refugees. They leave hunger only to stay hungry, because many of them wind up living in overcrowded camps that have limited food supplies. An average basic ration for refugees consists of only a pound of cornmeal, two ounces of beans, an ounce of oil, and a half ounce of sugar. This basic ration provides few nutrients.

Hazards multiply

The living conditions are also unhealthful because many refugee camps have poor sanitation, inadequate shelter, and low vaccination rates. Fatal diseases like tuberculosis and contagious diseases like measles often sweep through refugee camps. Death also frequently comes as a result of uncontrolled diarrhea caused by unsafe water, intestinal diseases and parasites, and lack of good medical care. Infants, children, pregnant women, and the elderly, who usually are already weakened by malnutrition, anemia, vitamin deficiencies, and other nutritional and health problems, are the ones most susceptible to death.

Starving Ethiopian refugees arrive in Kenya. Hunger is one of the reasons people flee their countries and abandon their homes.

Refugees, especially women and children, become vulnerable to long-term hunger when they leave their homes. Usually there is a higher number of children, the ill, the handicapped, and widows in a refugee population than would be found in a typical population. This is because the men might have gone to the cities in search of work or may have been killed or drafted to fight in an ongoing war. Thousands of children in a single camp may be orphaned or separated from their families. Refugee camps often grow haphazardly on the least-valuable land, leading to poor shelter, sanitation, and security. The absence of security leaves precious food supplies vulnerable to theft, a common occurrence in refugee camps.

One Ethiopian refugee in Somalia is quoted by the Bread for the World Institute in 1994 as saying: "During the early days in the camp, life was very bad. There was very little food, no clean water and a lot of diseases. Many people died."

During the decade between 1985 and 1995, hunger has resulted in terrible conditions at refugee camps in Ethiopia and the Sudan. During the 1984 and 1985 drought and famine in the

Horn of Africa (a region that includes Ethiopia and Somalia), the two main refugee centers in neighboring Sudan became "living nightmares," according to one refugee. More than 100,000 Ethiopian refugees crowded into a camp designed for only 5,000. In early 1985 as many as half of the children suffered from moderate or severe malnutrition, and 10 to 30 of every 1,000 people died each month. In another camp lived 7,700 people, of whom nearly 1,400 were children under the age of 5. At least 1 out of 8 of these children died during a single 2-month period, January to March 1985.

An equally important factor of this migration is its impact on the host countries. Host countries often set aside land for the use of refugees and in many cases provide food, water, shelter, sanitation, schools, and health services. The problem is that many of the host countries are poor themselves. Caring for the refugees puts a strain on their own people's food security because refugees

Sudanese refugees experience crowded conditions at a refugee camp in Ethiopia.

must naturally compete with them for jobs and food. For example, Malawi, one of the poorest and most densely populated countries in Africa, had given refuge as of February 1992 to about 980,000 Mozambican refugees of drought- and war-related hunger—about one-tenth of Malawi's population.

International aid agencies try to change the conditions in which refugees live. They increase food supplies to camps and improve health conditions. However, it is often impossible to determine exactly how many people live in the camps, which means that there might not always be enough food to go around. It is also a major expense for donor organizations to provide the necessary supplies to refugees. Finally, especially in those areas in which there is armed conflict, it may be dangerous and difficult to transport food to the camps.

Mozambican refugees in Malawi. Malawi, itself a poor country, housed enough Mozambican refugees to equal about one-tenth of its population.

While malnutrition, disease, poor social conditions, and migration alter conditions for people in many Third World countries, the effects are likely to be felt for many generations to come. Hunger does not only destroy people, it also destroys nations. The most productive people—those between the ages of childhood and old age—are unable to work productively if they are starving. A nation has no future when its younger generation dies or is permanently damaged by hunger.

A nation without a future

In no country is the future more in doubt than in Somalia. There, during the years 1991 to early 1993, about a quarter of a million children under the age of five died of famine. Somalia's famine was caused by war-driven food blockades. Robert Buchanan of OXFAM America walked through the camps where people tried to get food during that period. "When I traveled the camps," he told the author, "I saw infants up to about six months, and then I wouldn't see any children from six months to five years of age. The impact of this ten to fifteen years from now will be devastating."

The devastation occurs in any country in which there will be fewer adults to have babies and keep the population steady. It also means there will be fewer adults to contribute to the economic strength of their country and fewer adults to grow food on farms. This almost guarantees that the children who do survive malnutrition and reach adulthood will struggle for the rest of their lives against hunger.

3

Environmental Causes of Hunger

HUNGER HAS MANY causes, and at least some of them have to do with the environment. The amount of sun and rain and the quality of soil and water are all directly tied to the earth's ability to grow food. It follows that sudden or dramatic changes in the natural environment can limit food-growing possibilities and may even disrupt food-distribution systems. Earthquakes, floods, and deforestation, or clearing forests from the land, all bring change to the natural environment. Whether this change or upheaval occurs naturally or is brought on by human hands, it can lead to disaster for human populations. Some countries can recover from environmental disasters more quickly than others can. In a population already struggling to feed, clothe, and care for itself, the result of environmental upheaval is often hunger.

Natural disasters

Natural disasters such as floods, drought, earthquakes, cyclones, and hurricanes can temporarily knock out food production, storage, and distribution systems even in developed, industrialized countries. This was evident after Hurricane Andrew swept through southern Florida in Au-

(Opposite page) An elderly cyclone survivor prays as his sons clean up the debris of their shattered home. Environmental disasters are a major cause of hunger.

45

gust 1992. A quarter of a million people lost their homes and businesses, and property damage totaled $20 billion. Since most food and water supplies were damaged or destroyed in the hurricane, $11.1 billion in emergency aid was trucked in by military convoy, along with huge tents designed to serve as temporary shelters. Although the hurricane uprooted people's lives—some permanently—most people had food to eat and water to drink within twenty-four hours of the storm's passing.

Poor countries are less able to deal with disasters of this magnitude. When natural disasters strike in the developing nations of the Third World, they often wipe out food supplies, bridges, roads, and irrigation systems and destroy farmlands. On April 30, 1991, a cyclone hit Bangladesh, killing 125,000 people and destroying virtually all of the nation's crops. Without food and without money to buy food elsewhere, millions faced starvation. Mass starvation was avoided only with the help of other countries.

A cyclone hit this village near the coast of Bangladesh in 1991, killing 125,000 people and destroying food supplies. Mass starvation was avoided through the help of other nations.

Piles of animal bones reveal the severity of a drought that wiped out animal populations and endangered humans in Ethiopia in 1974.

Foreign-aid donors sent $250 million in food, supplies, equipment, and cash.

Natural disaster can also arrive in the shape of insect and pest infestations. Locusts, crickets, rats, and worms can destroy whole fields of crops within days. Infestations on this scale can also lead to hunger. Ethiopian crops have been plagued by locusts and armyworms every two years for the last twenty years, says OXFAM's Buchanan. The most recent locust and armyworm infestation occurred in 1994, destroying 75 to 80 percent of the grain harvest, including maize and sorghum, in the province of Eritrea alone.

Drought

Perhaps the most devastating natural disaster that results in hunger, if only because it tends to be long lasting and recurring, is drought. Droughts have been associated with hunger almost every year of the last few decades. Drought is a long period during which rainfall is practically nonexistent. Crops fail from lack of water, and livestock die because they have nothing to eat.

Between 1979 and 1981 widespread drought in Africa left at least ninety-nine million people—

26 percent of the total population—without adequate food and consequently malnourished. In 1982 the drought affected about twenty-five countries. By 1984 the situation had worsened, and conditions deteriorated rapidly in Ethiopia, the Sudan, and the Sahelian zone. Of the thirty to thirty-five million people affected, at least ten million abandoned their homes and land to search for food and water. Farming suffered terribly during this time. According to OXFAM's Buchanan:

> Farmers still have not recovered. The farms are not back up to the point where they have all the resources they need. The farmers are living so close to the edge economically. What they need is five to ten years of favorable weather conditions so they can get back on their feet, and they have not been blessed with that. Yet, each year they hope it will be a better season.

The Sahelian zone

In the Sahel region of Africa drought has dried up water holes and turned what was rocky farmland into land of little use. The Sahel is a belt across Africa south of the Sahara Desert and north of the rainy regions of tropical Africa. It is roughly four thousand miles long and one thousand miles wide. The Sahel includes the countries of Mauritania, Mali, Niger, Burkina Faso, Chad, the Sudan, and the Central African Republic.

History records great droughts in the Sahel, periods in which the annual monsoon rains did not come or there was too little rainfall. Drought struck in the early 1970s and again in the 1980s. In normal times rainfall in the Sahel belt of sub-Saharan Africa varies no more or less than about 20 percent from an average of eight inches a year.

When the drought struck the Sahel region in 1972, rainfall dropped to less than 70 percent of the norm. Sand buried the crops. Because of the sand and the lack of water, farmland became un-

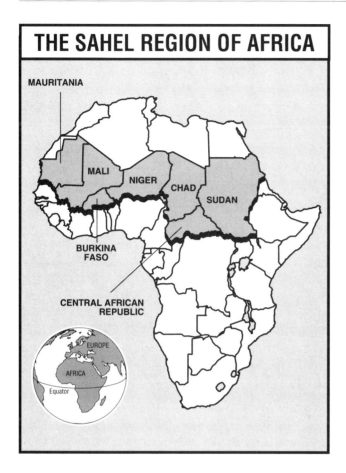

THE SAHEL REGION OF AFRICA

MAURITANIA

MALI

NIGER

CHAD

SUDAN

BURKINA
FASO

CENTRAL AFRICAN
REPUBLIC

EUROPE

AFRICA

Equator

suitable for growing new crops. Without the ability to grow crops, people left. Villages and settlements became ghost towns. During the second year of the drought one city in Mauritania's Sahel belt received only 1.6 inches of rain—about one-fifth of its normal yearly rainfall. Animals died or were sold as the people fled to the cities. In 1984 the rains failed again. The effects of that drought, felt hundreds of miles away in Chad, caused hunger for more than half of that country's population.

In the typical pattern of the Sahel region, drought was followed by torrential rainfall. The problem of reaching the drought-affected people of the Sudan was then complicated by floods that washed away bridges and roads. Almost one mil-

Starving cattle wander in search of food in drought-stricken Senegal in 1973. Experts are trying to predict drought to ease and prevent the terrible destruction wrought on animals and people.

lion people throughout the region needed food relief as a result of the drought.

Scientists have developed an early-warning system that enables them to predict when drought and floods might occur. By measuring climatic conditions and estimating the yields of farms, scientists can prevent the world from being caught off guard when these events do occur. They cannot stop natural events, but at least relief operations can be put in place in advance.

Human effects on the environment

Some human actions can alter the environment as much as any natural disaster and with similar results. By cutting down too many trees, by overgrazing livestock, and by using poor farming practices, people degrade the land so that crops cannot grow. This is most devastating in poor countries, which may already have a limited number and variety of crops, little or no surplus, and little or no money for buying food elsewhere.

The connection between hunger and the environment is especially obvious in Africa. The continent not only faces a hunger crisis, it faces an environmental one as well. Buchanan explains:

> In Africa, people are forced to grow crops on very marginal lands that are overcultivated. They chop down trees for fuelwood. And as the population expands, people are forced to farm on less-fertile land and to exhaust it more quickly. They are not in the position to allow natural resources to regenerate because their survival is at stake.

As a result, soil erosion is fast becoming Africa's number one environmental problem. Its effects can be felt across the continent as people struggle to plant crops in soil that has few nutrients and is unable to hold water. This complicates efforts to grow enough food for Africa's population of 654 million people.

Soil erosion results from practices such as

overgrazing of livestock, clearing trees for fuel and cultivation, and not allowing soil to rest, or lie fallow, every other growing season. These practices are not limited to Africa; they occur in countries around the world. But in Africa fertile soil is becoming more scarce. About 130 million acres of farmland are at risk of irreversible erosion.

Deforestation

Millions of rural and urban households in developing countries depend on fuelwood for cooking their meals and heating their homes. This wood usually comes from nearby trees. Dead wood is collected first. When dead wood is gone, live trees and bushes—and sometimes even the roots—are cut, leaving entire patches of barren forestland. The process of clearing the land of trees is called deforestation. Deforested land erodes easily because nothing remains to hold the soil in place. Soil washes down hillsides during floods, often destroying villages and farmland at the same time.

Deforestation costs India thirty to fifty million tons of food grains each year because erosion has made the land useless for farming. In Africa soil erosion from deforestation has reached critical levels, with farmers pushing farther into deforested hillsides. In Ethiopia, for example, soil loss occurs at a rate of about 2 billion cubic yards a year, with about 10 million acres of highlands considered to be irreversibly degraded.

Commercial lumber operations also contribute to this problem. Deforestation by lumber companies is increasing all across Asia, Africa, and Latin America. Southeast Asia's logging industry accounts for nearly 90 percent of the world's $7 billion annual trade in tropical lumber products. Large-scale lumbering is the primary cause of the frequent floods that devastate Bangladesh.

A Gambian farmer and his oxen plow a millet field that has been destroyed by drought. Soil may already be badly damaged in such areas because of poor farming practices.

Somali refugees in Kenya collect wood to cook food. Because Third World villagers use wood for everything, including shelter and cooking, they overharvest forests, leaving barren soil behind.

Bangladesh used to suffer a destructive flood every fifty years or so. By the 1980s the country was being hit with major floods—which wash away farms and rice paddies—every four years.

Overgrazing

Erosion can also be caused by overgrazing of animals. Much erosion in Africa is caused by large herds of domestic animals, such as cows, sheep, and goats, overgrazing on limited plant growth. This plant growth is important for holding soil in place so that it is not carried away by the wind and rain onto farmland. Because livestock production is important to Third World countries for dairy products, meat, and transportation, shepherds often risk plant life for the lives of their animals.

In times of drought herders bring their cattle, goats, sheep, horses, and camels to well sites, where they graze until no grasses are left. "All it takes is enough animals concentrated around a water hole to destroy it," says Thomas R. DeGregori, a professor of economics at the University of Houston. "It looks like a bomb crater when

Third World exportation of wood to developed nations has led to widespread deforestation. Deforestation can increase the negative effects of natural disaster, such as flooding.

they are done." When plant life near a water hole has been consumed by animals, the water hole is then at risk of being filled in by blowing soil. This means that people suffer the loss of drinking water as well as the ability to water crops.

In the last twenty years governments have tried to counteract this damage. Regulations now exist to limit herd populations, for instance, though DeGregori says the herders do not always follow these regulations.

Poor farming practices

The livelihood of Third World people depends to a large extent on agriculture. Whatever reduces the land's fertility—its ability to support plants—and productivity makes that livelihood even less stable. In a desperate need to feed their families, farmers often resort to farming practices that might provide food from only one harvest instead of annually. They strain to make a living on land that is infertile and no longer able to withstand

A shepherd grazes his sheep in the Congo. The overgrazing of sheep can cause soil erosion and permanent loss of native grasses.

such natural stresses as drought and heavy rain. By increasing production the farmers hurt the land even more. They cultivate land that should be allowed to rest and restore its nutrients through fallowing. They also strip the roots of harvested crops in a process called mining so they can feed their livestock. These roots could serve as mulch, a ground cover that holds in moisture. Mulch protects plants from freezing temperatures and prevents erosion.

As a result of these practices, nutrient-containing topsoil is blown away by winds or washed away by rain every year. This is not easy to replace. Depending on climatic conditions, it takes from one hundred to four hundred years to generate a single centimeter of topsoil.

Limiting genetic diversity

It is not just soil-damaging farm practices that can destroy food supplies, however. Monoculture also endangers the future of crops. This means that farmers use only seeds that are bred to resist pests and drought, causing older varieties to be forgotten and creating a lack of genetic diversity. When farmers switch to the new popular varieties, the older plants, which were well adapted to local conditions, can easily disappear. The genes of the older, hardier plants might have been used to breed future drought-resistant plants, but the practice of monoculture can threaten that possibility.

Seed banks have been set up worldwide to stop this genetic erosion. International agencies have worked to establish a worldwide network of eight banks that holds many varieties of seeds for twenty-five important food crops, such as wheat. And individuals who recognize the danger of losing genetic diversity have also begun saving seeds. People like Kent Whealy of the Seed Savers Exchange in Decorah, Iowa, believe that whole food supplies could be wiped out if these seeds are not saved. "You never know what important characteristic an older vegetable type has that might be needed to save a wheat field someday," Whealy says.

Desertification

However, even a diversity of seeds cannot survive as long as deforestation, overgrazing, and poor farming practices continue to increase desertification, which is the most critical form of land degradation in the Third World. Desertification—the process whereby land becomes desert—is a natural process that takes place through changes in the climate, but it also results from land mismanagement due to poor farming and ranching practices and lumbering. Desertification is the permanent decline of the potential of land to support plants.

When desertification sets in, farm tools can barely scratch the surface to make holes for seeds. And there is very little topsoil in which plants can grow roots. When roots cannot take hold, wind erodes whatever topsoil remains. Blowing soil not only leaves behind a degraded area, but can also bury and kill vegetation where it settles. It will also fill drainage and irrigation ditches.

Arid, or excessively dry, land adapted for farming—usually through irrigation—makes up about 43 percent of the total land area of the world. When arid land reverts to desert, hunger follows. Most crops cannot survive in the parched landscape, so harvests fail. Arid landscapes are so fragile that they break down quickly. A drought can mean catastrophe. It is estimated that twenty-five thousand square miles of the world's arable land, or land that is fit for cultivation, has turned to desert each year because of human misuse. The situation is most serious in the dry and semiarid regions of Africa and Asia.

The U.N. Environment Program warns that at least 11.3 billion acres—35 percent of the earth's land surface—are in various stages of desertification. More than 850 million people live in these areas. The problem is worldwide, but the greatest harm is to those areas already experiencing the greatest hunger—Africa, Asia, and Latin America. Today one-sixth of the total world population—135 million people—is threatened by desertification.

Halting environmental destruction

Governments and private organizations are trying to find ways to lessen the impact of the environmental causes of hunger. Droughts, floods, and other natural disasters may not be wholly preventable. But disruptions in food production and distribution because of some natural disasters can be diminished through such preventative measures as irrigation and early-warning systems.

Efforts to change human habits and practices

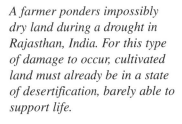

A farmer ponders impossibly dry land during a drought in Rajasthan, India. For this type of damage to occur, cultivated land must already be in a state of desertification, barely able to support life.

A photograph of the Tunisian terrain reveals the effects of drought and erosion. Overuse of land throughout the Third World has led to similar soil erosion.

take time, however. These efforts require education, such as teaching farmers to use less destructive farming practices. To diminish water-caused erosion on hillsides, for instance, farmers are taught contour farming. In this method, horizontal rows of grass are grown between rows of crops. When crops are harvested, the grass roots hold down the soil that would otherwise wash away when it rains.

All these efforts require money. Since June 1992, when development experts met at the U.N. Conference on Environment and Development, U.N. funds have been set aside to help preserve land in Third World countries. Treaties have been designed to protect the diversity of crops and to examine ways to end desertification.

Finally, halting the environmental causes of hunger will require thought, dedication, and attention to the practical needs of different peoples worldwide.

4

The Deepest Roots of Hunger

HUNGER'S DEEPEST AND most tangled roots grow in the soil of social, cultural, and political structures. From these structures arise poverty, war, and uncontrolled population growth. All of these have some part in causing or aggravating hunger in countries around the world. U.N. secretary-general Boutros Boutros-Ghali recognized this in 1993 when he said, "Famines are not caused by natural disasters alone. They arise all too often from man-made causes, like warfare and poverty."

Poverty

Poverty, some experts say, is the single greatest cause of hunger. Today 750 million people worldwide, about one-third of the population in developing countries, live in poverty. This is also close to the number of people who suffer from malnutrition. And the number of people living in poverty and without enough food seems to be growing.

"Unless there is a change in the current trend, the number of people living in absolute poverty—unable to afford minimal food and other needs—will continue to grow," says World Bank president Lewis T. Preston. "Hunger and malnutrition

(Opposite page) A famine-stricken woman awaits the arrival of food aid in 1992. Political, social, and cultural structures often lead to or worsen hunger.

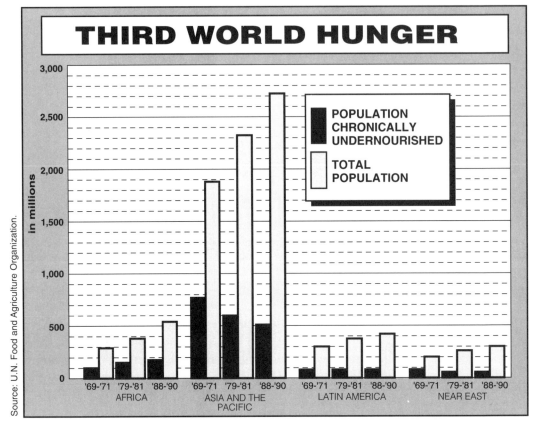

Source: U.N. Food and Agriculture Organization.

are the most devastating problems facing the world's poor."

The majority of the poor are concentrated in two regions—southern Asia and sub-Saharan Africa. These are people living on less than one dollar a day, and most of them suffer from hunger. Eight hundred million poor people live in Asia. Forty-six percent of the world's poor people live in southern Asia alone. In Africa there are about 250 million poor people.

Since most people in developing countries are farmers, they need land on which to grow food for their own use or to sell. Those who actually own land often have small, poor-quality plots that barely support plant life. So they are caught in a cycle of being unable to grow food sufficient to feed their families and to sell at market, thus earning inadequate money to pay for more seeds or more land. Frequently, to earn money to support themselves, they are forced to sell parcels of their land to family members or wealthy landholders. The result is more and more people farming on smaller and smaller plots, which eventually destroys the fertility of what little land they have.

The troubles of farmers

As a result, the Food and Agricultural Organization reports a serious decline in the amount of fertile land farmed by each farmer. The vast majority of farm households in developing countries must make do on farms of two hectares (approximately five acres) or less. In Asia and the island nations of the Pacific, the amount of productive land worked by each farmer in the early 1960s was about one hectare. By the year 2000, FAO estimates, that number will be barely three-quarters of a hectare per farmer. In Africa the 1961 to 1965 rate of 2.37 hectares per farmer is expected to drop to 2.04 hectares by 2000. And in North Africa and the Middle East, the rate is predicted to fall from 2.89 hectares in the early 1960s to 2.21 by the end of the century.

If farmers were able to get loans during hard times so they could buy seeds, fertilizers, and tools, they might not have to sell their land. But little or no financial credit is available to improve conditions on small farms in the hunger-belt region. Small-scale producers and enterprises—farmers, tradespeople, and traders—account for 30 to 70 percent of the labor force in some developing nations. In many countries even a loan as small as thirty dollars could help someone start a business or keep a farm going. But commercial banks are not usually set up to serve the needs of the small-

A farmer sprays maize with pesticide in Africa. Farmers in Third World nations are farming increasingly smaller plots of land.

scale producers. Their credit needs are usually too small to be cost-efficient for most banks.

All of this translates into joblessness. When farmers have little or no land to farm, they become unemployed, further adding to their hunger. The International Labour Organization reports a widespread rural employment crisis in developing countries. In Bangladesh an estimated 26 percent of the total rural labor force in 1977 were landless and another 11 percent owned so little land that they were almost wholly dependent on low-paying wage labor. This picture has surely worsened since then.

Wage-labor jobs can rarely be found in rural areas, leading many landless farmers—usually men—to cities in search of work. There people do all kinds of jobs, such as basket weaving, carpentry, snake charming, and housecleaning. Those who manage to find work earn minimal wages. A fourteen-hour workday in a truck parts shop in Calcutta, India, for example, pays about

Afghan refugees look for work in Pakistan. Many farmers who have lost their land search for work in the city. When no jobs are available, hunger and poverty increase.

one dollar. More often, however, there is no work to be found.

In 1987 the World Food Council found evidence of dramatic increases in the number of unemployed people in many countries. Records for India showed an increase of ten million unemployed between 1980 and 1985. In Indonesia and Thailand the unemployment rate increased 6 to 7 percent annually in the 1970s, a trend that continued into the 1980s. In Brazil the number of unemployed more than doubled between the early 1970s and early 1980s.

Some experts believe that the hunger problem in many parts of the developing world can be improved just by an increase in employment, rather than by an increase of food production. M.S. Swaminathan, former director of the International Rice Research Institute, states that "fighting the 'famine of jobs' will be as essential as maintaining adequate food production for the rest of the twentieth century."

Women's work

With men leaving home to fight in civil wars or to find work in the cities, family members must rely on women's earnings. Women contribute 60 to 80 percent of the gross national product in many countries, yet they are chronically underpaid and hold low-status jobs. Former U.N. secretary-general Kurt Waldheim said of women's roles in poor countries: "While women represent half the global population and one-third of the labor force, they receive only one-tenth of the world income and own less than 1 percent of the world property."

The spread of hunger in Africa is aggravated by the economic and political conditions of women. Women make up two-thirds of poor Africans. In Malawi alone, women do twice the work men do on maize, the country's staple, or principal, food

Women pick tomatoes in Yemen. Although women's labor produces almost half of the world's total food, the pay they earn is less than half of what men earn.

crop, an equal amount on cotton—the chief export crop—and still have their domestic chores to do at home. Another study in Zambia found that the size of the harvest depends on the number of daylight hours women could spend on farming.

Women's labor produces almost half of the world's total food. However, food experts believe that Africa's declining food security is due to the fact that land titles are assigned only to individual heads of household, with the assumption that these are husbands. Further, farm equipment is given only to men and credit is provided only to landowners, i.e., men. Such economic practices are devastating to the future of farming in Third World countries. If the male head of household is not around, either because he is working in a city, fighting in a war, or has died, a woman's hands are completely tied, and she can make no financial improvements to her family's life. This discrimination against women has eroded the productivity of Africa's women farmers, all of which helps keep families living in poverty and without food.

Fleeing civil strife

Poverty-stricken people in developing countries often become trapped by hunger due to civil wars, as well. Sometimes farmland is used as a battlefield, so no crops can be planted. Other times people may flee their homes with whatever possessions they can carry. They can take only limited food and water, and often they escape to areas where food and water are also in short supply or not available at all. When large populations of people migrate to another country it is almost inevitable that hunger will be the result.

In the summer of 1994 it took just five days for 1.7 million refugees of civil war in the African nation of Rwanda to pour across the border to Goma, Zaire. This was the largest exodus, or mass departure, of a population of refugees ever recorded. Goma's population is only twenty thousand. To feed the masses, eight million tons of food a day were needed—an incredible financial strain for the government of Zaire and aid organizations.

Because there was a lack of clean drinking water, as many as eighteen hundred people died each day from the infectious disease cholera before foreign aid arrived. The United States sent

Refugees flee Kigali, Rwanda, with whatever possessions they can carry. Civil wars often lead to hunger because people flee to neighboring nations that may have difficulty feeding their own people.

nearly a half billion dollars in food, purified water, and medicine to the Rwandan war refugees. President Bill Clinton said at a White House conference: "We have delivered more than 1,300 tons of equipment, food, water, and medicine. We have increased safe water production and distribution from nothing to 100,000 gallons a day."

However, because there was an enormous refugee population, people waited in lines for rationed clean water, sometimes for twelve hours, to get only enough water for a family for one day. The next challenge was food. A July 27, 1994, *New York Times* article said, "Relief shipments provided a food ration of ten and a half ounces of corn or rice a week per person, which lasts a family of four only a day." Refugees also quickly depleted, or exhausted, their life savings by buying the limited foods available at greatly inflated prices. Ten dollars enabled twenty-year-old Marie-Claire Mukamusitau to buy two tablespoons of sugar or ten high-protein biscuits, according to an August 3, 1994, article in the *New York Times*.

Food as a weapon

Even before the mass exodus from Rwanda, food was becoming scarce there. That is because food was being used as a weapon of war. Using food as a weapon is a frequent tactic in war. One side might destroy crops, often by slashing and burning them, or steal from or detain food deliveries intended for the other side in hopes of weakening the opponent and gaining the advantage. An August 8, 1994, *New York Times* article stated: "Combatants do not shrink from using food as a weapon, either by blocking relief convoys or engaging in 'slash and burn' techniques of warfare."

This type of behavior goes on in warring countries worldwide. Desperately needed shipments of

A U.N. peacekeeper in Sarajevo inspects boxes of humanitarian aid to make sure that they contain only food and medical supplies. Serbian soldiers blocked food shipments to Bosnian Muslims in 1993.

food, medicine, and other supplies have been routinely delayed, hijacked, or stolen in the Bosnian war in what was formerly the European nation of Yugoslavia. In early 1993, for example, Serbian soldiers prevented U.N. food convoys from reaching 100,000 Muslims trapped in besieged towns in eastern Bosnia, as *Time* magazine reported in its March 1, 1993, issue.

Similar events took place in Rwanda in May 1994. With civil war raging in the capital of Kigali, food supplies were running dangerously low. More than 200,000 people in Rwanda were in need of food assistance. Fighting had prevented deliveries of food and water to all but 3,000 of the 12,500 people staying in a U.N. refugee camp there. About 11,000 tons of corn, beans, and oil sat in 7 warehouses near the city, but rebel armies kept the food away from the people. As a result, more than 500 children under the age of 10 were without new supplies of food for a week.

Squeezing the enemy

This use of food as a weapon was also the chief cause of famine in the Horn of Africa in 1988. The governments of Ethiopia and the Sudan had been fighting both each other and civil wars within their own countries in the northern provinces, where hunger was worst. A drought had already put millions of people in a famine situation. This made food an even more valuable weapon. The two governments prevented food shipments from reaching civilians in rebellious areas. Government officials denied relief agencies passage through government lines and in some cases threatened to bomb truck convoys carrying food. They banished foreign workers from many conflict areas and prevented them from entering others. This made it nearly impossible to learn how much food was needed, to hand it out, or to monitor its distribution. Officials prevented journalists from inspecting conditions, making it hopeless for accurate information to reach aid agencies and foreign governments that might provide help. They used food donations to help feed their armies, and in the Sudan, at least, the government-armed militia destroyed or stole food.

"It is shocking but true that if a famine situation develops in civil war zones, a government will try to use it to reduce the population of its rival," says OXFAM's Robert Buchanan.

According to a hearing by the U.S. Select Committee on Hunger, the Sudan received $72 million in U.S. food and development aid in 1988 to counteract the effects of both drought and war. Practically none of the food paid for with that money reached the people of the southern Sudan, according to relief workers. The famine victims lived in war zones. In some cases these victims were surrounded by millions of dollars of food shipments, yet relief agencies like the International Committee of the Red Cross were prevented from distributing this food to the most desperate people. This is because most of them lived outside areas of government control, and the rebels would not let the food reach them. At least five million people were threatened with terrible shortages of food in the Sudan.

In Ethiopia about one million metric tons of food were shipped by developed countries to help feed about nine million famine victims, most of which they never received. Civil war finally

A Sudanese policeman drives back a hungry crowd as they struggle to get at relief grain sent by the Save the Children organization in 1985.

ended in Ethiopia in 1991, although fighting in the Sudan continues.

Population growth

In the next decade population growth will probably add to world hunger problems. As the population grows, according to the World Hunger Program, so will the number of chronically malnourished people. The world's population, estimated at 5.6 billion in 1994, may reach 11.5 billion by the year 2150, and most of that growth is occurring in the world's poorest countries. At least 95 percent of the global population growth over the next thirty-five years will take place in the hunger-belt regions of Africa, Asia, and Latin America. For countries that already have a hard

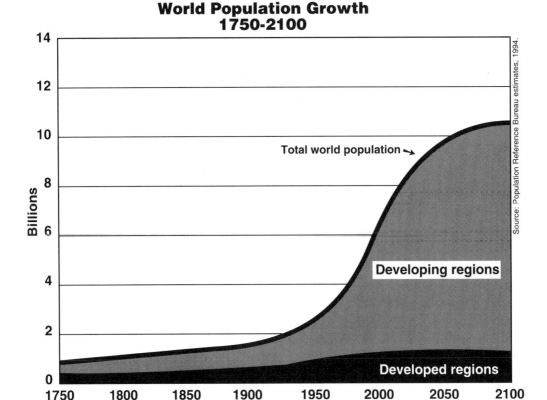

World Population Growth 1750-2100

Total world population

Developing regions

Developed regions

Source: Population Reference Bureau estimates, 1994.

time feeding their populations, growth on a scale of even 3 percent a year could add significantly to their food problems. This level of growth is already occurring in Namibia and in South Africa, and many other countries are not far behind.

In 1981 the United Nations recorded a population on the African continent of 481 million people. This number is predicted to top 800 million by the year 2000. Africa would have to increase its food production by 4 percent a year to meet the food needs of its increased population. But Africa's food production is growing by only 1 percent a year, which means that nations already struggling to meet their people's food needs will have an even greater struggle as populations grow. "When food supply grows slower than population," says Professor DeGregori, "a country is in trouble."

A task both fundamental and immense

Fighting the causes of hunger is no easy task. Some experts say the real answer to hunger lies in ending poverty. World hunger agencies are, therefore, targeting poverty as a means to end hunger. Boutros Boutros-Ghali says that since the overwhelming majority of the world's chronically undernourished people live in rural areas, and since poverty is a major cause of hunger, the search for solutions to the world hunger problem must start with the rural poor. "Enabling this segment of society to improve food security for their households greatly reduces the world hunger problem," he said. This task is both fundamental and immense.

If the population in African nations continues to grow at its current rate, many countries will have a difficult time feeding their people.

5

What Role Can Agriculture Play in Ending Hunger?

Agriculture can play a role in ending world hunger, but to have an impact on hunger, it must be sustainable. This means people must have the ability to grow their own food locally and on a long-term basis without needing constant money and assistance from others and without harming the land in food-growing regions. If this is to be accomplished it will probably take a combination of traditional practices and new ideas.

Efforts to develop new food sources in the 1960s led to what was called a new era of agriculture—the Green Revolution. During this period botanists, scientists who study plant life, came up with an idea they believed would end hunger. If a plant could be made to double the amount of usable food it made, they reasoned, the world food supply would also double. Many people believed this idea to be one of the most significant agricultural advancements in decades. The seeds that could accomplish this wonderful feat were called miracle seeds.

Dr. Norman Borlaug of the United States was the most widely known of the researchers who

(Opposite page) A woman waters tomato plants in Ghana. Sustainable agriculture is one important key to ending hunger.

Dr. Norman Borlaug was a key figure during the Green Revolution for his development of drought-resistant, high-yield grain seeds.

were trying to develop high-yield seeds. He won the Nobel Peace Prize in 1970 for his discovery. In the late 1940s he developed wheat and rice seeds that produced high yields and were also drought resistant. The benefits of this new generation of improved seeds were dramatic. The Green Revolution increased food production worldwide. Between 1950 and 1985 worldwide grain production grew at an average annual rate of 2.7 percent. Third World countries with famine problems showed a remarkable improvement in crop yields. Some fields produced three times as much grain an acre as in previous years. Wheat production in India doubled in just four years. In 1966 Borlaug expressed his excitement about the early years of the Green Revolution to Pakistan's secretary of agriculture: "Sir, one year ago we predicted that Pakistan could double its wheat production in five years. We now repeat that forecast."

The Green Revolution continued to meet with success during the 1970s. It was used not only in developing countries, but in industrialized countries as well. The U.S. corn output in 1975 was double that of 1960. India, the poorest country in the world, actually produced enough grain for its population in the late 1970s. By the mid-1980s Green Revolution seeds were used in half the world's rice and wheat fields, providing more than 50 million extra tons of grain. World grain population climbed from 631 million metric tons in 1950 to 1.65 billion metric tons in 1984.

No miracle cure

But the successes of the high-yield seeds did not end world hunger because they could not be sustained. The seeds required fertilizer, pesticides, irrigation, and machinery, which most farmers in poor nations could not afford. Poor farmers who tried to take advantage of the Green Revolution were unable to raise the money to buy the seeds, the fertilizer, the pesticides, or the equipment. As a result only wealthy farmers benefited from the new seeds. Their increased output caused an over-supply of grain that lowered the market price of wheat. Poor farmers could not increase their production to make up for the lower price, leaving them with many expenses and little or no profit.

The environment did not fare well either. Poor land was brought into production through the use of increased irrigation. This created a scarcity of water because it quickly decreased water supplies in many places in the world. Erosion from over-farming the land caused millions of acres to be withdrawn from production. Further, the use of chemical fertilizers, which was increased nine-fold between 1950 and 1984, had an adverse, or harmful, effect on water supplies. Some fertilizer washed into streams, ponds, and lakes, where it caused them to become overrun with plant life. This in turn took away the oxygen supply for fish. The result was that people's fish supplies were threatened.

During the Green Revolution, specially developed seeds (above) resulted in high crop yields but also required heavy use of costly and potentially harmful chemical pesticides and fertilizers (below).

One of the lessons of the Green Revolution is that agriculture alone cannot end world hunger. It can play a role in ending hunger, but that role must take into account the needs and lives of the people it is intended to help. And it will require open-mindedness to both new ideas and traditional methods.

Natural farming methods

Some traditional methods of farming, including multicropping, intercropping, fallowing, and crop rotation, have been used in countries around the world, and in some cases, for centuries. Where used, these techniques have resulted in high crop yields and healthy growing conditions.

Multicropping involves the use of a single piece of land for growing crops year-round. As one crop is harvested, another is planted, thus making full use of a single plot of land and favorable year-round growing conditions. Multicropping is especially useful with high-yield varieties because they mature faster, especially in the year-round warm climate near the equator. The idea of multicropping is not new; it has been practiced for at least six thousand years. In southern China, where the climate permits multicropping, three grain crops are often grown on the same plot of land each year.

Increased use of multicropping can add millions of tons of grain to world food output, simply because many crops are grown during the course of one year on the same farmland. Because it requires more labor, it can also create more rural jobs.

In intercropping, two or more crops are grown at the same time in alternating rows or right next to each other. For example, maize may be grown with beans. The maize stalk serves as a pole for the beans to climb, and the beans naturally in-

Beans and maize are inter-cropped in Kenya. Intercropping is only suitable for areas where most harvesting is done by hand.

crease the nutrients of the soil. The beans also provide the delicate maize flowers with shade. Modern farming, which relies on machines to harvest crops, could never take advantage of intercropping the way a traditional farmer can. The traditional farmer can walk through a field and handpick the beans without damaging the maize. A machine that could fill the same role would not be cost-effective.

Another traditional process is called fallowing, in which no crops are grown for a year or more. Leaving land idle, or fallow, is vital for maintaining soil fertility and moisture, especially in semi-arid regions. More than twenty-five million acres of western wheat lands in the United States are usually left fallow each year. Fallowing is also common in Canada, Australia, and Russia. Even though fallowing takes land out of production temporarily, it is necessary if the soil is to keep producing good crops. This practice helps stop land deterioration by giving the soil time to restore nutrients needed for healthy crop growth.

Pesticides can be used more sparingly if crops are rotated, by growing corn one year, perhaps, and wheat the next. This way pests would not have enough time to develop resistance.

These methods of farming all rely on the availability of farmland. In countries where fertile farmland is hard to find, but food supplies are short, people must find ways to farm on land that was previously thought to be unusable.

Of the more than 13 billion hectares of land in the world, the total amount of potentially cultivatable land is generally agreed to be about 3.2 billion hectares. Only about 1.4 billion are now being cultivated. Thus, the area upon which food can be grown could be more than doubled. The problem is that the richest, most available, and easiest land to farm is already being used. It costs thousands of dollars per hectare to drain or clear and irrigate new crop-growing land. Further, this land may never be as productive as the prime lands used now.

New technologies are constantly being developed that permit the production of food on land previously believed unusable. For example, fertile soil can be created where it did not previously exist by using composting, fertilizing, manuring, and many other techniques.

Current development programs have focused on carefully bringing new land under cultivation through irrigation projects. Another alternative is to increase the yield per acre of land already under cultivation, as was done during the Green Revolution. However, where climate and other conditions are unfavorable, what the land produces depends considerably on the availability of water, energy, and fertilizers.

Fertilizers

Food experts say that dependence on expensive fertilizers and potentially harmful pesticides must be reduced if farming is to play a part in ending hunger. If used improperly both pose a hazard to people, animals, and the environment. Concern about the long-term effects of commercial fertilizers, along with their rising costs, have prompted some scientists to look for alternatives. One method used widely is to plant a legume such as clover every two or three years. A clover crop can add 1,650 pounds of nitrogen to an acre of soil. Plants need nitrogen for growth; added nitrogen helps plants self-fertilize. A legume called winter vetch can be planted in cornfields in late summer and then plowed under in the spring. This would provide the soil with 133 pounds of nitrogen per acre.

Manure and other wastes, such as leftovers and garbage, are also being explored as sources of nutrients for crops. Manure improves the soil's water-holding capacity, reduces erosion, and adds beneficial bacteria and fungi at a much lower cost and in smaller quantities than does commercial fertilizer. A year's manure from one dairy cow, nine hogs, or eighty-four chickens yields as much fer-

A Peruvian farmer spreads manure on his potato crop. Much cheaper than chemical fertilizer, manure is more available and reduces erosion.

tilizer as farmers usually apply to an acre of corn in the United States.

There is plenty of manure available—an estimated 1.7 billion tons in the United States alone. The cost of transporting manure and spreading it makes most farmers prefer commercial fertilizers, which are also easier to use. But rising costs of commercial fertilizers will probably stimulate more interest in these natural fertilizers.

Pest control in the fields can also be improved. The natural enemies of pests can reduce pest numbers. Among the most successful are lintel wasps, which lay their eggs on the bodies of plant-eating insects. After a wasp larva hatches, it feeds on the pest and kills it. Several kinds of insect pests have been brought under control this way.

Plant breeders have already had some success in developing plants that resist pest attacks. This resistance is usually lost within five to fifteen years because pests develop a tolerance for the resistant qualities of the specially bred plants. So there is a constant challenge to develop new resistant varieties. Botanists have already created new products such as disease-resistant sugarcane.

Producing new kinds of foods is an idea that hunger experts hope could play a part in ending world hunger. Scientists are taking a look at nontraditional sources for foods with high nutritional value that can easily be grown and harvested. However, before scientists rely on new types of food, many of them are attempting to use what already exists. Some of these foods have not been tried before. Others have been replaced and forgotten over time. One of the goals of biotechnology—the use of living organisms to make valuable food—is to discover ways that humans can tap into unused sources of nutrients in the form of plants, animals, and even bacteria.

Among the six thousand or so plants that have been identified as having edible parts, there are

Hunger has led to a renewed interest in little-used grains, such as amaranth, once planted by the Aztecs.

some that, like the soybean, might become a major source of food in the future. There are other plants that once were used for food sources that have been almost forgotten. For example, grain amaranth and quinoa were among thirty-six infrequently grown plants that were cited in a 1975 publication, *Unexploited Tropical Plants with Promising Economic Value*, published by the National Academy of Sciences. Amaranth has more amino acids—the building blocks of protein—than most cereal grains.

The Aztecs once grew amaranth in abundance. Quinoa, whose grain is also rich in protein, was grown by the Incas. It is still grown today by the mountain people in Bolivia, Chile, Ecuador, and Peru, who grind the seeds for cake flour. Other forgotten varieties include a wild Australian cereal grass called *Echinochla turnerana; Zostera marina*, a grain-producing plant that grows in saltwater; and *Arracacia xanthorrhiza*, also

Quinoa, a grain once planted by the Incas and still popular in South America, may be another protein-rich grain that can be grown in African nations to end hunger.

known as the Peruvian carrot or apio. All of these have the potential to provide Third World countries with nutrient-rich, easily grown crops. Says author John N. Cole of amaranth in particular, "There are few, if any, grain crops as properly protein-rich as the amaranth."

The single-celled organisms blue-green algae may provide another source of food because they are high in protein. Food producers have experimented with algae and seaweeds from the ocean in high-nutrition food products. Blue-green algae are already grown on a small commercial scale in Hawaii, Thailand, Israel, and Taiwan. Although fairly expensive, they are sold in dried form and in tablets in health food stores for use as a protein supplement. But scientists hope that in the future the protein of blue-green algae can be used to enhance food supplies of people who are hungry.

New farming methods

In addition to new foods, new farming methods are being explored as well. The sea offers another source of food through fish and shellfish farming, or aquaculture. Aquaculture is an idea that has been around for a long time. In this process a water source, such as a pond, is created so that fish can be carefully bred without harming the environment or future fish populations. It requires a careful circulation system so that waste can be moved out of the water before it changes the environment of the fish.

The Chinese developed carp-farming techniques thousands of years ago. In the United States today farming of freshwater catfish and trout and of saltwater shellfish has been successful. Recently scientists at the Woods Hole Oceanographic Institution in Falmouth, Massachusetts, developed a method of fish farming that uses human sewage from a nearby treatment plant

Farmers in Thailand transplant rice seedlings. Plants that can be grown in salty water are also being studied for use in ending hunger.

as fertilizer for algae, which in turn nourish the oysters, fish, and edible seaweeds there. However, industrialized countries do not as yet rely on aquaculture for food. But fish is used to increase food supplies in many Asian countries and in some African countries, such as Lesotho, where the freshwater carp fish tilapia is common. The potential of fish farming as a means to fight hunger has not been fully realized. Terry Frady of the National Marine Fishery Services in Massachusetts explains that fish farming is like keeping an aquarium. It takes a lot of input and expense, but if it is done well, fish can grow hardily and plentifully. Most aquaculture, however, is still in the experimental stage.

Scientists are investigating water as a source in which to grow plant life as well. Hydroponics, the science of growing plants without soil, is another new farm method. Hydroponic farming consists of two primary methods, one using water, the other using gravel or coarse sand. Hydroponic farms could make use of the water supply from lakes and ponds without the need for soil or irrigation. All that is needed is the addition of the proper nutrients.

Plants that tolerate salty soil are being looked at for a method called saltwater farming. These plants are called halophytes. Salt-contaminated soil is a common problem in Africa. Contamination occurs when saltwater evaporates and leaves behind salt deposits in which crops cannot grow.

In Idaho Charles W. Robbins, a U.S. Department of Agriculture soil scientist, has created sordan. This is a patented mix, or hybrid, of sorghum and Sudan grasses from Africa. Sordan could be a valuable crop for repairing the salty soils in Africa so that food crops can be grown. Sordan actually repairs certain types of sodium-rich soils. Its roots secrete an acid that dissolves soil salts. Water can then penetrate the bricklike ground and let plant roots take hold. A few Oregon ranchers have used sordan to repair soil. "Within three years they were growing alfalfa," says Robbins.

Finding a balance

These agricultural methods of ending world hunger are still in the experimental stages. If they are one day combined with natural farming methods that have worked for centuries, food experts believe there is a good chance they can help to end world hunger.

However, recent history has shown that for every new agricultural development there is a possibility that the environment will be harmed. What is needed most is a sensitivity to human needs and to the delicate balance of nature.

6

What Is Being Done to End World Hunger?

THE OXFORD COMMITTEE for Famine Relief (OXFAM) was formed by volunteers in Oxford, England, during World War II to fight famine in Nazi-occupied Greece. The war-driven famine there killed about 450,000 people before OXFAM shipped donated food to the area. Since that time shipments of wheat, rice, beans, and cooking oil have been available from many agencies in times of crisis for all countries in the world.

Today emergency food aid is the most common form of assistance given to nations experiencing hunger. The total annual food aid coming from worldwide agencies to sub-Saharan Africa alone is now worth more than $1 billion. More than 15 million people in 209 countries received emergency food aid from projects approved by the U.N. World Food Program in 1988. In 1989 there were 46 emergency food projects: 29 in Africa, 5 in Asia, 8 in the Near East, and 4 in Latin America.

International efforts to eliminate hunger have led to other forms of aid, too. Economic development assistance, nutrition education, and food-

(Opposite page) Ethiopians line up for food assistance, still the most common form of assistance given to hungry nations.

for-work programs are among the efforts under way in dozens of countries around the world. These and other projects are being run with the help of nations, as well as numerous private agencies and organizations.

Those who devote themselves to ending hunger understand better than most that solutions to the world's hunger problems will not come easily. Hunger is a complicated problem with many causes that will take many different ideas and efforts to end. "There are no simple solutions to these complex issues," says Professor DeGregori, "because there is rarely a single cause of hunger. Since in most cases it is a combination of war, population, and environmental conditions, it will take a combination of solutions to end hunger from area to area."

Emergency and long-term aid

One of these efforts to end world hunger is distributing emergency food aid from organizations like OXFAM. Providing food aid requires careful timing so that food shipments arrive at a food-poor area early enough to avoid famine, but not so early that food surpluses bring down the price of local produce.

In these situations the governments in famine-prone countries use their early-warning systems for more than just monitoring rainfall. Together with the early-warning systems of the U.S. Agency for International Development and the U.N. Food and Agricultural Organization, economic trends are monitored as well. These organizations learn a lot by watching local grain markets. When the price of grain goes up and the price of livestock goes down, this is a sign that there may be a food crisis. People tend to sell their livestock in times of food shortage because they do not have the food to feed them. They also

need the cash from the sale of the livestock to buy food for their families.

The goal is to uncover potential famine areas before people run out of food supplies. Timing is critical, because once people sell their assets and leave their villages in search of food, it is difficult and costly to get them to go back home. Their health must first be rehabilitated after a prolonged food shortage. Then, in order to grow food on their farms again, they need such things as new seeds and farm tools.

Food-aid organizations do not always interpret the early-warning signs correctly. "Timing is very crucial, and the donor community has some difficulty timing it right," said OXFAM's Robert Buchanan. But this system has convinced aid communities that most famine situations can be avoided.

Food aid is just one of the ways that organizations are battling world hunger. While private organizations are geared to respond immediately to

Bags of wheat flour are unloaded in Lesotho. Organizations that supply grain attempt to interpret the warning signs of famine in order to prevent hunger.

Farmers plant pine seedlings as part of a reforestation project. Reforestation decreases soil erosion and renews overused soil.

disasters, their emphasis is on small, long-term development projects aimed at the poorest and neediest. Organizations strive to help improve the economy of developing countries so that such countries will not have to rely on food aid as much in the future. They do this through long-term development projects.

"The biggest argument about fighting hunger is that unless you have economic growth taking place, it is very hard to address the basic poverty question that prevents people from getting food," says Robert Kates, former director of the World Hunger Program.

There are many different foreign-aid programs that address all aspects of development that have a bearing on food and hunger. One of the most popular of these is a food-for-work program, pioneered in 1961 by Church World Services, an international relief agency of American Protestant churches. Under this program a recipient country pays laborers in food rather than cash. The U.N. World Food Program provides most of its aid as food-for-work on various public projects such as road repairs. Food-for-work jobs assist only the poorest people, those who have no employment at the time. The public works projects are supposed to support rural development and agriculture by constructing or improving an area's infrastructure, or systems of public works, such as roads, irrigation canals, dams, and terracing or reforestation schemes to halt erosion. Many food-for-work laborers are women of the poorest households, who often support children as single parents.

Since 1993 OXFAM has funded a food-for-work program in Eritrea, a province of Ethiopia. Workers in the community are building a river dam that will allow this drought-affected area to grow food year-round through six hundred irrigated farm plots. The project will take several years. During that time the Eritrean government has agreed to pay a few thousand able-bodied workers with food. However, 80 percent of the 1994 harvest was lost due to drought so that food-aid needs have soared there. OXFAM provided the government with $50,000 to purchase food for people working on the project and for those who are unable to work, such as children and elderly people.

Success of programs like these is not guaranteed. Sometimes the plans do not take into account the cultures and living conditions of the people they are intended to help. Some projects have included dams that displaced thousands of people, roads that cut through forestland, and factories that produced goods few people could afford. Careful measures that take into account the differences from country to country must be maintained.

Immunization

Ending hunger will also require education in the fields of health, nutrition, and family planning. Education in these areas can provide important tools for individuals and families. Knowledge, along with assistance from other countries, can increase the chances of survival of even the most vulnerable groups.

One focus of governments in the last decade has been providing immunizations for children in order to decrease susceptibility to disease. For instance, Colombia began an immunization campaign in 1984. The result was that more than 60 percent of the children under the age of five years were vaccinated by the following year.

Vaccination programs will go a long way toward preventing childhood diseases and protecting malnourished children from almost certain death. "For example, just a decade ago, 2.5 million children died from measles annually," says James Grant, executive director of UNICEF. "This number has been cut to about 1 million per year due to cheap, readily available vaccines."

Nutrition and family planning

The number of children who die from whooping cough has been cut in half, to about 300,000 annually, as a result of vaccinations. And no cases of the paralyzing disease polio have been reported in the Western Hemisphere since 1992.

Targeted nutrition intervention is also being used in Third World countries to increase children's chances of survival. Even when food is available, children often become malnourished because their parents do not understand what nutrients a child needs for healthy growth. A baby that reaches six months for example, needs other foods in addition to breast milk, or the baby will become malnourished. Through classes sponsored by aid organizations like the World Health Program, mothers are taught about their children's food requirements. A particular emphasis

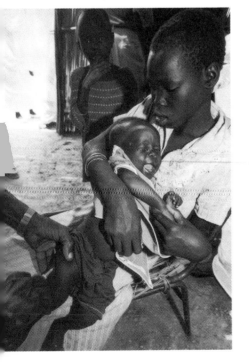

A Sudanese infant is vaccinated against measles. Third World children, because of poor diets, are especially susceptible to such diseases, which can quickly become fatal.

An Afghan refugee learns about good nutrition. Educational programs that focus on nutrition and family planning provide people with information for improving health and determining the size of their families.

is on teaching mothers about their babies' nutritional needs. "An essential piece [of ending hunger] is behavioral change, particularly with respect to infants, so that they are fed often enough and are weaned properly," says Judy McGuire, a senior nutritionist at the World Bank. The combination of reasonably good nutrition and immunizations raises the chances of survival for most children.

Family planning can also be a tool for combatting hunger. Having control over when it has children allows a family to have only as many as it can feed and improves the chances that those children will survive.

Birth control usage is not high in most Third World countries. There are several reasons for this. Many women do not use birth control because they do not have access to it. In instances when it is available, it may be used incorrectly. Some families also have personal, cultural, or religious beliefs that prevent them from using birth

In a Planned Parenthood clinic in Jamaica, a doctor explains how the birth control device known as an IUD works.

control. Therefore, family planning campaigns sometimes encounter resistance. However, family planning remains a tool like any other—available for use by those who learn to use it and wish to use it.

Botswana

With the help of various aid programs, many countries have shown remarkable success in ending hunger during this century. Since 1900, seventy-five countries have ended hunger. Forty-one have accomplished this since 1960. One of these countries is Botswana in sub-Saharan Africa.

Like other African countries, Botswana has experienced huge population growth at a rate of 2.5 percent a year. The country currently has 1.2 million people. Until the 1980s Botswana's population was mostly poor. The average person earned $290 a year.

When Botswana achieved independence from Great Britain in 1966, it was emerging from a terrible drought. The United Nations listed it as one of the world's least-developed countries. With the help of food-for-work programs and food programs for school children, infants, and breast-feeding women, Botswana avoided mass famine. Ketumile Masire, president of the Republic of Botswana, says that at the height of the drought, the country was able to feed almost one-third of its population because of these aid programs.

Botswana is more fortunate than some other countries. It is one of the world's leading diamond producers. This mineral now provides more than 75 percent of the country's revenue and in the last decade has helped raise the average annual income per person from $290 to $1,690. Profits from the diamond industry have been used to provide health care, roads, education, food supplies, dams, and irrigation systems. The country saves enough money to pay for three months of food for its entire population in case of drought. This food supply helped Botswana avoid famine when it suffered another drought, one that lasted for six years, from 1981 to 1987.

President Masire says that the country has a three-point plan to fight hunger. At the national

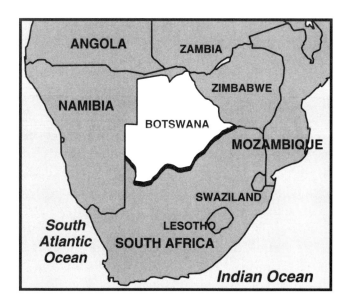

level the government pays for imported food by exporting minerals and manufactured products and by promoting tourism. At the local level the goal is to ensure that every family has sufficient basic income to buy the food it needs. This means helping poor people through food-for-work programs. Finally, the government distributes food to pregnant and breast-feeding mothers, children under five, and those in schools to ensure the minimum nutrition requirements are met. While the country is still struggling with a fast-growing population, which can mean less food to go around, currently only 10 to 15 percent of the population suffers from malnutrition. "This is low for Africa," says President Masire, "but not low enough. My country will continue to spend about $14 million each year to develop food programs."

Is the end of hunger in sight?

The decrease of hunger in countries like Botswana is encouraging to those who are trying to achieve similar results in other countries. In its 1980 study *Agriculture: Toward 2000*, the Food and Agricultural Organization concludes that hunger can be abolished. The study marks a turning point in the global fight to eliminate hunger. It recognizes that for the first time in history the world now has the agricultural, technological, and financial resources to end hunger forever. Through a combination of early-warning systems, national and global food reserves, and food-for-work programs, the end of famine is well within sight. Hunger experts agree that meeting the emergency food needs of Third World countries is an attainable goal by the year 2000.

According to the Food and Agriculture report: "The end of hunger is now a possibility but it is not a promise. We need to see what is missing in the global effort to fight hunger."

A key to ending hunger is ending poverty. The poverty rate in China has been steadily dropping and hunger, once a serious problem in China, has practically disappeared.

What is missing, many experts say, is a way to end poverty. Yet, poverty is slowly decreasing in some parts of the world. The evidence of this can be seen in Asia. Asian countries have made steady progress in reducing poverty and hunger over the last twenty years. The World Bank reports that in many nations the portion of the population living in poverty has declined significantly. Between 1970 and 1990 the poverty rate in China fell from 33 to 10 percent, or from 275 million to 100 million people. In Indonesia the poverty rate fell from 60 to 15 percent, or from 70 million to 27 million people. India's poverty rate dropped from 48 percent in 1978 to 25 percent in 1992. But the number of poor Indians increased to 210 million because of population growth.

A number of countries that had depended on food aid have become self-sufficient through changes in economic policies. Among them are India, Indonesia, and Vietnam. Bangladesh's basic grain production has kept pace with population growth since the mid-1980s. These successes are seen as a decreasing trend in food poverty. Hunger experts say food poverty has probably diminished by half in the last thirty years, though this rate of decline has slowed dramatically in recent years.

Marshaling efforts

Because international organizations believe the end of hunger may be attainable, they are marshaling efforts to intervene on behalf of those who are deprived. In 1989 twenty-three experts from fourteen countries designed a statement of priorities for reducing hunger in developing countries. The gathering of experts was sponsored by the Brown University World Hunger Program. Its statement is called *The Bellagio Declaration: Overcoming Hunger in the 1990s*. This declaration focuses on both immediate and long-range actions to lessen hunger, though the emphasis is on what can be accomplished quickly.

It has four targets. These are to eliminate death by famine, cut malnutrition in half for mothers and small children, eliminate iodine and vitamin A deficiencies, and end hunger in half of the poorest households. The first three goals, the experts agreed, can be done—as has been demonstrated in many places—by relatively inexpensive, practical methods. The fourth goal, to end hunger by changing the economic status of the poor, is more difficult to achieve.

Nonetheless, success stories like those of Botswana and other southern African countries, including Zimbabwe, Zambia, and Malawi, which all have been able to feed their populations despite a drought in 1993, can serve as examples of what developing countries can do to fight hunger. While more than half of these countries' crop yields was destroyed in the drought, their governments found innovative ways to feed their

people. In Malawi the government gave food away to the population. In Zambia the government kept food prices low. In all of these countries millions of tons of food were imported, and southern African governments cooperated in making sure it could be distributed.

Other efforts to end hunger will require major changes in population growth, environmental degradation, and economic growth in Third World countries. Robert Kates says that global food production needs to expand three-fold over the next sixty years, particularly in regions that could not take advantage of the Green Revolution. World population must stabilize by then, which means that the rate of increase in Third World countries must begin to decrease. Most importantly, according to Kates, is that all of these changes must include the voices of the people in the places that make up the bulk of the world's hungry.

Mozambican refugees in Malawi receive food aid. Such aid remains a vital part of curbing hunger.

Glossary

agricultural biotechnology: The science concerned with creating new foods through modern genetics.

aquaculture: The cultivation of the natural produce of water such as fish and shellfish.

chronic hunger: A long-term lack of the proteins and calories a human needs for survival.

deficiency disease: A disease caused by a lack of vitamins, minerals, or other nutrients essential for good health and normal body functions.

deforestation: The clearing of trees and forests.

desertification: The loss of land flexibility in arid areas.

fallow: Cultivated land that is allowed to lie idle during the growing season.

famine: An extreme scarcity of food that puts a population at risk of starvation.

food poverty: When individual households cannot meet their food needs despite an availability of adequate food supplies.

food security: Access by everyone at all times to enough food to maintain an active life.

Green Revolution: The significant increase in agricultural output due to the introduction of high-yield varieties of grains in the 1960s.

hectare: A metric unit equal to almost 2.5 acres.

hydroponics: The science of growing plants without soil; usually in water or gravel or coarse sand.

intercropping: To grow two or more crops at the same time in alternating rows or right next to each other.

malabsorptive hunger: When a body cannot absorb the nutrients from food that has been consumed.

malnutrition: A lack of nutrients, such as fat and protein, needed for human health.

monoculture: Using only one plant type for each fruit and vegetable, resulting in a loss of genetic diversity.

multicropping: The use of a single piece of land for growing crops year-round; as one crop is harvested, another is planted.

starvation: An extreme form of malnourishment in which the body digests vital tissues and organs.

Third World countries: Countries in Africa, Asia, and Latin America having high illiteracy rates, high birth rates, limited schools, crude communication and transportation systems, and an inability to meet their food needs.

undernourishment: A lack of adequate calories.

Organizations to Contact

The following organizations are internationally known for their efforts to fight world hunger. More information can be obtained directly from each organization.

Bread for the World Institute
1100 Wayne Ave., Suite 1000
Silver Spring, MD 20910
(301) 608-2400

Bread for the World Institute is a national political movement among Christians in the United States. It seeks to inform, educate, and motivate concerned citizens for action on policies that affect hungry people. It develops education resources and activities, including its annual report on the state of world hunger, policy briefs, and study guides.

International Labour Organization (ILO)
1828 L St. NW, Suite 801
Washington, DC 20036
(202) 653-7652

The ILO sponsors many studies about hunger, poverty, and development from the viewpoint of the opportunities, wages, and working conditions of labor, including self-employed entrepreneurs in farming and nonfarming enterprises.

OXFAM America
26 West St.
Boston, MA 02111-1206
(617) 482-1211

OXFAM America is a development and disaster assistance organization cooperating in a worldwide network known as OXFAM. The organization promotes economic and food self-reliance, responds to emergency needs of political and natural disaster refugees, and supports development programs. The organization publishes a newsletter and produces and distributes pamphlets, books, and films.

United Nations Children's Fund (UNICEF)
3 United Nations Plaza
New York, NY 10017-4414
(212) 326-7035

For more than forty years UNICEF has supported countries to improve their resources for children, to establish priorities, and to reach the neediest children. UNICEF promotes the well-being of children in 127 countries and territories.

United Nations Food and Agricultural Organization (FAO)
1001 22nd St. NW, Suite 300
Washington, DC 20437
(202) 653-2400

FAO is the oldest, largest, and most diversified of the U.N. organizations. Its purpose is to do research and provide technical assistance to increase agricultural production, promote human nutrition, and create better conditions for rural populations.

World Health Organization (WHO)
525 23rd St. NW
Washington, DC 20037
(202) 861-3200

WHO is linked to efforts to end hunger through its role in advancing nutrition and pediatrics research, training, and using the health sciences to reduce major public health problems.

World Hunger Program
Brown University
Box 1831
Providence, RI 02912
(401) 863-2700

The Alan Shawn Feinstein World Hunger Program at Brown University is the only major university research center whose goal is to eliminate hunger. It was established in 1985. The program's research is focused on three areas: the history of hunger, analyses of how trends within major world regions will affect hunger, and assessments of the values, policies, and institutions needed to prevent hunger.

Suggestions for Further Reading

Nathan Aaseng, *Ending World Hunger*. New York: Franklin Watts, 1991.

John Christopher Fine, *The Hunger Road*. New York: Macmillan, 1988.

Christopher Gibb, *Food or Famine?* Vero Beach, FL: Rourke Enterprises, 1987.

Elizabeth S. Helfman, *This Hungry World*. New York: Lee and Shepard, 1970.

The Hunger Project, *Ending Hunger: An Idea Whose Time Has Come*. New York: Praeger, 1985.

Patricia L. Kutzner, *Contemporary World Issues: World Hunger*. Santa Barbara, CA: ABC-CLIO, 1991.

Frances Moore Lappé, *World Hunger, Twelve Myths*. New York: Grove Press, 1986.

Steven Manning, "Why Africans Go Hungry," *Scholastic Update*, November 6, 1992.

Laurence Pringle, *Our Hungry Earth: The World Food Crisis*. New York: Macmillan, 1976.

Leslie Withers and Tom Peterson, eds., *Hunger Action Handbook*. Seeds Magazine, 1987.

Additional Works Consulted

Elizabeth Antebi and David Fishback, *Biotechnology Strategies for Life*. Cambridge, MA: MIT Press, 1985.

Isaac Asimov, "Futureworld: The Future of the Sea," *Boys' Life*, November 1991.

Audubon, "Environmental Refugees: A Moveable Famine," March/April 1993.

John Bierman, "The Victims," *McLean's*, May 20, 1991.

Raymond Bonner, "Wisdom of Urging Rwandans' Return Dividing Officials," *The New York Times*, July 29, 1994.

Liza N. Burby, "Heirloom Seeds," *Country Journal*, March/April 1992.

————, "Scarce and Historic Seeds Are Being Preserved as Heirlooms," *The New York Times*, September 6, 1992.

Business America, "Coming Back to Life," July 29 and August 12, 1991.

Susan Chira, "Women Campaign for New Plan to Curb the World's Population," *The New York Times*, April 13, 1994.

John N. Cole, *Amaranth from the Past for the Future*. Emmaus, PA: Rodale Press, 1979.

Carole Collins, "Pro-Democracy Forces, Rules Clash in Kenya and Malawi," *National Catholic Reporter*, May 22, 1992.

Robert Cooke, "Millions Are Still Desperate," *Newsday*, January 18, 1994.

Kimberly A. Crews, *Human Needs and Nature's Balance: Population, Resources, and the Environment.* Washington, D.C.: Population Reference Bureau, 1987.

Thomas R. DeGregori, Book reviews, *The Journal of Economic Issues,* September 1993.

————, *Technology and the Economic Development of the Tropical African Frontier.* Cleveland, OH: Case Western Reserve University Press, 1969.

Jack Doyle, *Altered Harvests.* New York: Viking Penguin, 1985.

The Economist, "The Green Counter-Revolution," April 20, 1991.

Arlene Eisenberg, Heidi Murkoff, and Sandee Hathaway, *What to Eat When You're Expecting.* New York: Workman Publishing, 1984.

James E. Ellis, "Can Biotech Put Bread on Third World Tables?" *Business Week*, December 14, 1992.

J.R.S. Fincham and J.R. Ravetz, *Genetically Engineered Organisms.* Toronto: University of Toronto Press, 1990.

Orville L. Freeman, "Meeting the Food Needs of the Coming Decade," *The Futurist*, November/December, 1990.

Roy Gutman, "Defying Death," *Newsday*, December 21, 1993.

Mike Hulme and Mick Kelly, "Exploring the Links Between Desertification and Climate Change," *Environment*, July/August 1993.

Hunger: Annual Report on the State of World Hunger. Silver Spring, MD: Bread for the World Institute, 1990, 1992, 1993, 1994.

Michael Ignatieff, "The Four Horsemen Are Here to Stay," *World Press Review*, July 1991.

E.J. Kahn Jr., *The Staffs of Life.* Boston: Little, Brown, 1984.

May Mederios Kent, *World Population: Fundamentals of Growth.* Washington, D.C.: Population Reference Bureau, 1990.

John M. Krochta, "Innovations for Tomorrow's Foods," *USA Today*, January 1991.

Eugene Linden, "Will We Run Low on Food?" *Time*, August 19, 1991.

Donatelle Lorch, "Fighting in Rwanda Capital Blocks Food Distribution," *The New York Times*, May 26, 1994.

———, "What Began as a Mission of Mercy Closes with Little Ceremony," *The New York Times*, March 26, 1994.

George R. Lucas Jr. and Thomas W. Ogletree, eds., *Lifeboat Ethics: The Moral Dilemmas of World Hunger*. New York: Harper and Row, 1976.

Jean L. Marx, *A Revolution in Biotechnology*. New York: Cambridge University Press, 1989.

Gary E. McCuen, *World Hunger and Social Justice.* Hudson, WI: GEM Publishers, 1986.

R. Monastersky, "Satellites Expose Myth of Marching Sahara," *Science News*, July 20, 1991.

Lucile F. Newman, *Hunger in History: Food Shortage, Poverty, and Deprivation.* Cambridge, MA: Basil Blackwell, 1990.

Newsday, "Rwandan Exodus," July 15, 1994.

Walter Olesky, *Miracles of Genetics*. Chicago: Childrens Press, 1986.

Dele Olojede, "Death Descends," *Newsday*, July 22, 1994.

———, "Low-Impact Aid Effort," *Newsday*, July 29, 1994.

Josephine Ouedraogo, "Sahel Women Fight Desert Advance," *UNESCO Courier*, March 1992.

Jane Perlez, "At Rwandan Camps, Life's a Bit Bearable," *The New York Times*, August 3, 1994.

Popular Science, "Plants with a Taste for Salt," April 1991.

Tajpertab Rajkumar, *The Struggle to Survive in the Third World*. Bombay, India: Jaico Publishing House, 1991.

Janet Raloff, "Desalinization, the Microbial Way," *Science News*, November 30, 1991.

Robert Rodale, *Save Three Lives: A Plan for Famine Prevention*. San Francisco: Sierra Club Books, 1991.

Nafis Sadik, "World Population Continues to Rise," *The Futurist*, March/April 1991.

Eric Schmitt, "U.S. Vows to Stay in Somalia Force Despite an Attack," *The New York Times*, September 26, 1993.

Ismail Serageldin, "International Conference Targets Scourge of Hunger," *World Bank News*, November 18, 1993.

Gayle Smith, "The Hunger," *Mother Jones*, September 1991.

Pitirim A. Sorokin, *Hunger as a Factor in Human Affairs*. Gainesville: University Presses of Florida, 1975.

William K. Stevens, "Poor Lands' Success in Cutting Birth Rate Upsets Old Theory," *The New York Times*, January 2, 1994.

Bruce Stutz, Fred Pearce, and Brad Warren, "The Landscape of Hunger," *Audubon,* March/April 1993.

Patrick E. Tyler, "Nature and Economic Boom Devouring China's Farmland," *The New York Times*, March 27, 1994.

U.S. House Select Committee on Hunger. *Ethiopia and Sudan: Warfare, Politics, and Famine*. Hearing, July 14, 1988.

Vivienne Walt, "Sudan, an Eerie Echo of Somalia," *Newsday*, April 25, 1993.

Michael Wines, "U.S. Sending Force of 200 to Reopen Rwandan Airport," *The New York Times*, July 30, 1994.

World Food Programme Journal, Rome, Italy, October/December 1993.

"World Hunger Awareness, Affinity, Action." Curriculum unit for grade eight, sponsored by the Alan Shawn Feinstein World Hunger Program at Brown University, Providence, RI, 1991.

Index

About the Author

Liza N. Burby is the author of two nonfiction books for young adults. She is also a book editor and a frequent contributor to the *New York Times* and numerous consumer magazines. Her specialties are social issues and profiles of people.

Picture Credits

Cover photo by Gianni Giansanti/SYGMA
AP/Wide World Photos, Inc., 12, 17, 29, 35, 47, 50, 86
The Bettmann Archive, 8, 31, 94
FAO photo, 56, 81
FAO photo by C. Errath, 75 (bottom)
FAO photo by D. Barker, 64
FAO photo by F. Botts, 57, 71, 72, 97
FAO photo by F. Mattioli, 78, 82
FAO photo by I. de Borhegyi, 80
FAO photo by John Isaac, 36
FAO photo by M. Sinko, 61
FAO photo by M.T. Palazzolo, 30
FAO photo by P. Pittet, 15
FAO photo by Peyton Johnson, 52 (bottom), 84
FAO photo by R. Cannersa, 53
FAO photo by S. Bunnag, 75 (top)
FAO photo by Y. Muller, 51
ICRAF photo distributed by FAO, 77
Reuters/Bettmann, 6, 22, 44, 46, 58, 65, 67, 69, 92
UN photo, 10
UN photo, issued by FAO, 90
UN photo/Peter Magubane, 20
UNHCR/A. Hollmann, 23, 34, 37, 42, 93, 99
UNHCR/B. Press, 38, 40, 52 (top)
UNHCR/H. Gloaguen, 62
UNHCR/M. Amar, 41
UNHCR/N. van Praag, 24
UPI/Bettmann, 9, 74
WFP/FAO photo by G. Tortoli, 89
WFP/FAO photo by P. Vaughan-Whitshead, 26